## STEP UP TO

# GCSE MUSIC

## Get up to speed with stave notation and the other core requirements in just two weeks

**PAUL TERRY**

Picture credits: p63; Royal Scottish National Orchestra © Tom Finnie
p64; A typical rock band © Aija Lehtonen/Shutterstock.com
Cover and book design: Fresh Lemon Australia
ISBN: 978-1-78558-175-5

Exclusively Distributed By

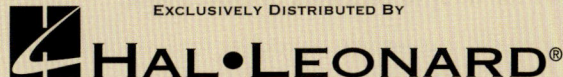

Copyright © 2016 Rhinegold Education, a part of HAL LEONARD LLC
International Copyright Secured   All Rights Reserved
No part of this publication may be reproduced in any form or by
any means without the prior written permission of the Publisher.
Visit Hal Leonard Online at
**www.halleonard.com**

**Contact us:**
Hal Leonard
7777 West Bluemound Road
Milwaukee, WI 53213
Email: info@halleonard.com

**In Europe, contact:**
Hal Leonard Europe Limited
42 Wigmore Street
Marylebone, London, W1U 2RY
Email: info@halleonardeurope.com

**In Australia, contact:**
Hal Leonard Australia Pty. Ltd.
4 Lentara Court
Cheltenham, Victoria, 3192 Australia
Email: info@halleonard.com.au

# Step Up

This book has been designed to get you up to speed with the musical understanding you'll need in order to get the top grades in your GCSE, whichever board you are studying. It should be used in combination with the dedicated study guide for your particular course.

**It is split into two sections: Theory and Knowledge. The 14 theory sessions start from the very beginning and take you through the essentials of stave notation, the source code of Western music. By the time you see this tune in session 13 …**

… you'll be able to decode the notes and discover the musical tricks that make it the most recognised song in the English language.

The Knowledge section takes you through the conventions, terminology and historical background that will allow you to get to grips with whatever your GCSE course throws at you. A few of the topics may not apply to the particular exam you will be taking. The 'Test your knowledge' section (Activity 22), which begins on page 66, introduces a short piece of music in its entirety and tests you on a range of topics that you have studied in this book.

## Beyond the exam

**An understanding of music theory and stave notation doesn't just help you to pass an exam, it allows you to take control of your musical life and opens the door to centuries of great music.**

If you can notate your music, it gives you the power to develop it and grow as a composer. It means you can get your music performed live, and it also means that you can import your scores into programs like GarageBand, Cubase and Logic and create tracks using all your favourite editing tools.

The notated scores for many of the great works in the history of music are available online to download for free. No one who can read stave notation ever has an excuse for running out of ideas!

# STEP UP TO GCSE MUSIC

## Theory

| | | Page |
|---|---|---|
| Session 1 | The stave | 4 |
| | The treble clef | 5 |
| Session 2 | The bass clef | 7 |
| | Leger lines | 8 |
| Session 3 | Time values | 9 |
| | Bars and time signatures (1) | 12 |
| Session 4 | Beaming notes and grouping rests | 14 |
| | Triplets | 17 |
| Session 5 | Bars and time signatures (2) | 18 |
| | Tied notes | 20 |
| Session 6 | Tones and semitones | 21 |
| | The scale and key of C major | 22 |
| Session 7 | Degrees of the scale | 23 |
| | Accidentals | 24 |
| Session 8 | Major keys and key signatures | 26 |
| Session 9 | Minor keys and minor scales | 31 |
| Session 10 | Modes and other scales | 34 |
| Session 11 | Intervals | 36 |
| Session 12 | Chords | 38 |
| Session 13 | Cadences and chord progressions | 42 |
| Session 14 | Modulation and tonality | 44 |

## Knowledge

| | |
|---|---|
| Terms and signs | 47 |
| Musical structures | 53 |
| Texture | 56 |
| Compositional devices | 58 |
| Voices and instruments | 60 |
| Historical periods | 64 |
| Test your knowledge | 66 |

| | |
|---|---|
| Answers | 68 |
| Index of terms | 71 |

# Session 1

## The stave

**Music is written on a set of five lines called a stave. Notes can be written on the lines (which actually means that a line passes through the note) or in the spaces between the lines. The notes are read from left to right, like words in a book.**

If a note sounds higher than another note we say it is higher in **pitch** and it is written in a higher position on the stave. If a note sounds lower than another note, we say it is lower in pitch and it is written at a lower position on the stave.

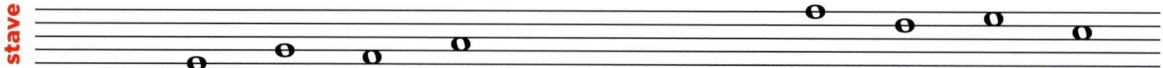

The shapes on the stave above are **note heads**. They are ovals, not circles, and should be written clearly so there is no doubt which line or space they are on.

## Letter names of notes

The pitches of notes are named after the first seven letters of the alphabet, from A to G. These are called the **letter names** of notes.

As we go through the alphabet, the pitches get higher:
A, B, C, D, E, F, G. After G, start again from A to go still higher in pitch. If we go backwards through the alphabet (G, F, E, D, C, B, A) the pitches get steadily lower.

The jump from one note to its neighbour, such as F to G, is called a **step**. Look at the diagram below. Can you see that A is one step higher than G and one step lower than B?

### STEP UP

It will help you to quickly work out the names of notes that go down in pitch if you are good at saying the musical alphabet backwards ('G F E D C B A').

## The treble clef

**A clef is written at the start of every stave to show how the letter names of notes fit on the lines and spaces.**

The **treble clef** ( 𝄞 ) is used for high notes. It curls around the second line up to indicate that this is the line for G. It began life many hundreds of years ago as a capital letter G, which over the centuries became more and more curly.

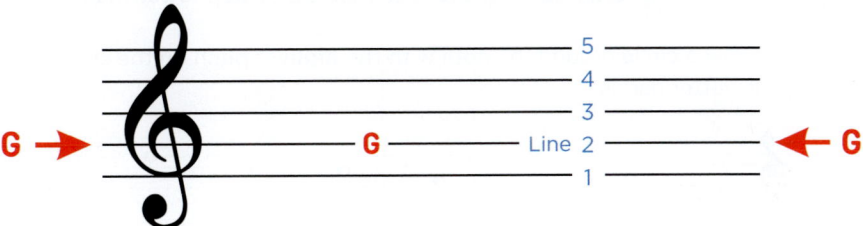

Now we know the line for G, we can work out where all the other letter names fit on the stave. Don't forget that the note that is a step higher than G is A:

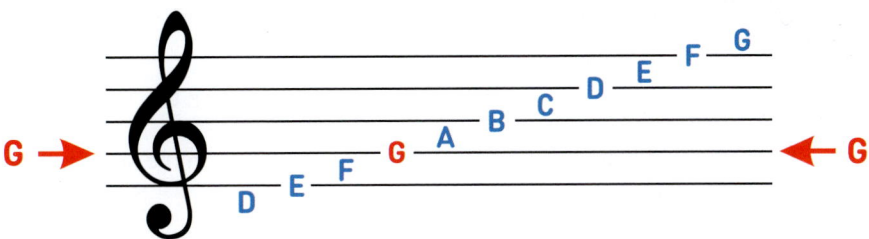

The notes in the four spaces spell **FACE**, reading up from the bottom. Some people like to learn the names of the notes on the five lines (**EGBDF**, reading up from the bottom) by remembering a sentence such as **E**very **G**ood **B**oy **D**eserves **F**ootball.

However, if you remember that the treble clef curls around the G line, it is easy to work out any letter name by just going through the musical alphabet as you count the lines and spaces from G:

- A step **up** to the line or space immediately above a note goes to the next letter in the musical alphabet (G to A, A to B, B to C and so on).

- A step **down** to the line or space immediately below a note goes to the previous letter in the musical alphabet (C to B, B to A, A to G and so on).

The G just above line 5 and the D just below line 1 must just touch the lines and not float above or below them.

# SESSION 1

## ACTIVITY 1

1. Which pitch does the treble clef indicate on a stave?

2. What is the letter name of the note that is one step **higher** than D?

3. What is the letter name of the note that is one step **lower** than A?

4. Draw a circle around the note with the **highest** pitch on the stave below and give its letter name.

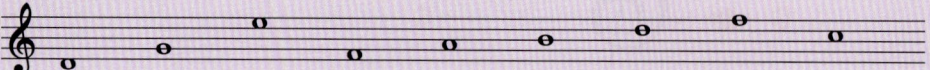

The letter name of the note with the highest pitch on this stave is

5. Draw a circle around the note with the **lowest** pitch on the stave below and give its letter name.

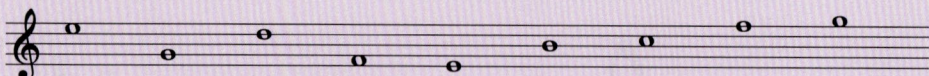

The letter name of the note with the lowest pitch on this stave is

6. Draw a circle around two notes next to each other on the stave below that are one step apart.

7. To find out why Edward felt ill, decode the following message by writing the letter names of the notes on the lines below the stave.

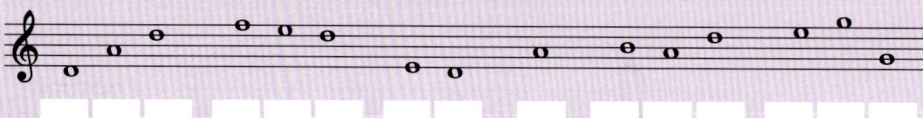

8. Write the named notes on the stave below, using 𝅝 for each one.

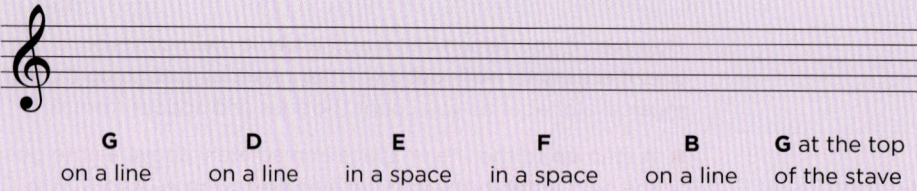

| G | D | E | F | B | G at the top |
| on a line | on a line | in a space | in a space | on a line | of the stave |

Remember, when we say that a note is 'on a line' we mean that a stave line passes through the note head.

# Session 2

## The bass clef

The **bass clef** ($\mathcal{9}:$) is used for low notes. It curls around the fourth line up of the stave to show that this is the line for F (a lower F than either of those in the treble clef shown on page 5). It was once a capital letter F, but now the sideways strokes have shrunk to just two dots.

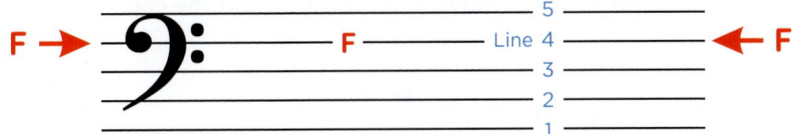

Now we know the line for F, we can work out where all the other letter names fit on the stave. Remember, the note which is a step higher than G is A:

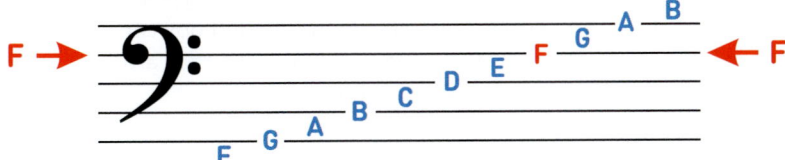

Some people like to learn the names of the notes in the four spaces (**ACEG**) by remembering a sentence such as **A**ll **C**ows **E**at **G**rass. However, if you remember that the bass clef fits around the F line, it is easy to work out any letter name by just going through the musical alphabet as you count the lines and spaces from F.

## ACTIVITY 2

**1.** Which pitch does the bass clef indicate on a stave? ☐

**2.** Draw a circle around the note with the **lowest** pitch on the stave below and give its letter name.

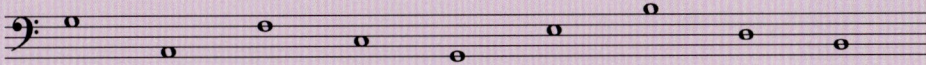

The letter name of the note with the **lowest** pitch on this stave is ☐

**3.** To find out what frightened Lucy, decode the following message by writing the letter names of the notes on the lines below the stave.

☐☐☐☐ ☐☐☐ in her ☐☐☐☐ on the ☐☐☐

**4.** Write the named notes on the stave below, using o for each one.

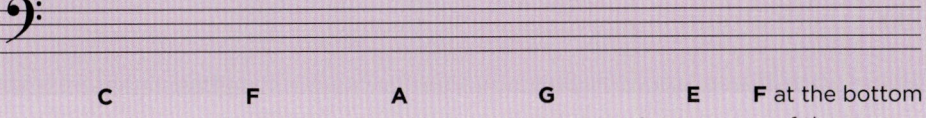

C in a space    F on a line    A in a space    G in a space    E in a space    F at the bottom of the stave

## SESSION 2

## Leger lines

**If a note is too high or too low to fit on a stave, we use leger lines. These are short extra lines above or below the stave. They are the same distance apart as the stave lines.**

Separate leger lines must be drawn for each note that needs them, but you don't need to use leger lines for notes that sit in the spaces immediately above and below the stave, such as the note at the end of this example:

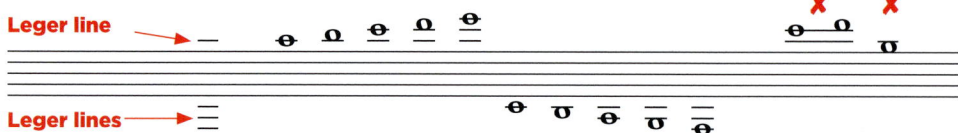

The next example shows how notes in the treble clef follow on from those in the bass clef as pitch rises. The notes in the shaded box can be written in either clef and sound the same whichever clef they are written in. The note in the middle is called **middle C**:

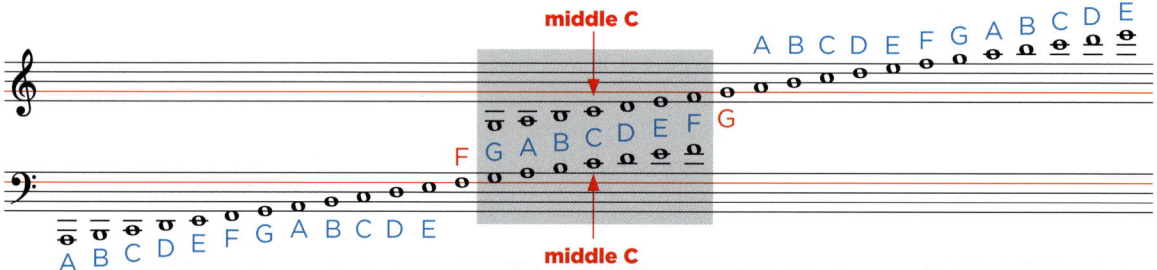

### ACTIVITY 3

1. Write the letter names of these notes on the lines below the stave. Then circle the **highest** and **lowest** notes on the stave.

2. Rewrite these notes in the treble clef so that they sound at the **same** pitch. The first note is given.

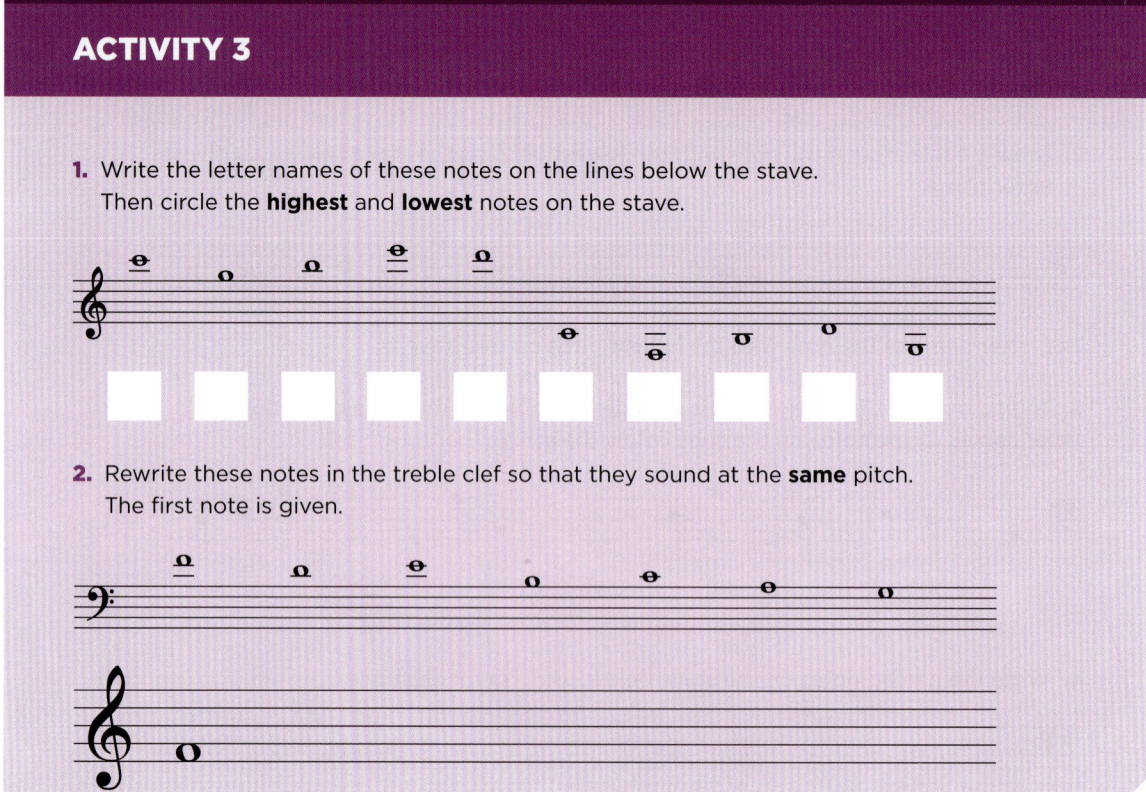

# Session 3

## Time values

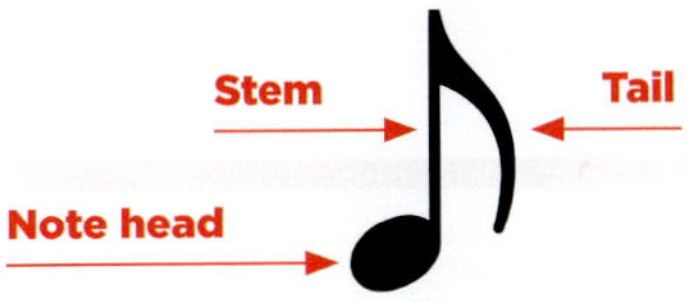

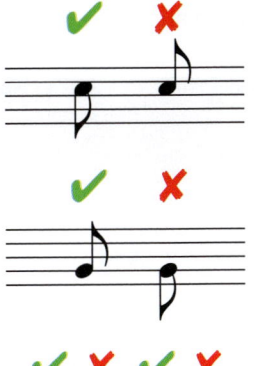

The length of a note is called its **time value** and is shown by the shape of the note. So far in this book we have used only a semibreve (whole note), which has a hollow note head (o). Other notes may have stems and tails, as shown left.

In music, a silence (called a **rest**) can be just as important as a note. For every note there is a rest of the same length. In the table below, the English terms for time values are shown in bold and their widely used American equivalents are shown in brackets.

| Name | Length | Note | Rest |
|---|---|---|---|
| **Semibreve** (whole note) | 4 beats | o | 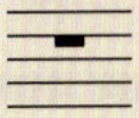 |
| **Minim** (half note) | 2 beats | 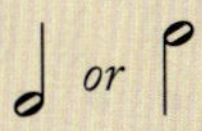 ♩ or ♩ |  |
| **Crotchet** (quarter note) | 1 beat | 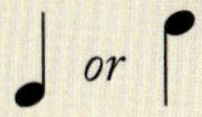 ♩ or ♩ |  |
| **Quaver** (eighth note) | ½ beat | 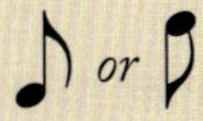 ♪ or ♪ |  |
| **Semiquaver** (16th note) | ¼ beat |  ♬ or ♬ | 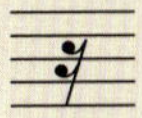 |
| **Demisemiquaver** (32nd note) | ⅛ beat |  ♬ or ♬ | 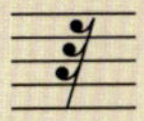 |

- Notes on and above the middle line of the stave normally have stems that go **down** from the **left** of the note head.

- Notes below the middle line of the stave normally have stems that go **up** from the **right** of the note head.

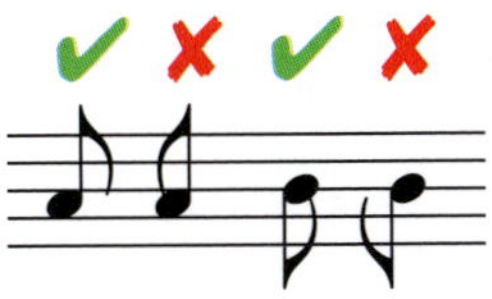

- Tails of short notes are **always** to the right of the stem, whether the stem goes up or down.

Rests should be positioned vertically on the stave as shown in the table above. Semibreve rests must hang from the fourth line up and minim rests must sit on the middle line.

The 'hooks' of a rest symbol always sit in spaces on the stave. The number of hooks is the same as the number of tails on a note of the same length. For instance, a semiquaver note has two tails and so a semiquaver rest has two hooks.

### STEP UP

Semibreve and minim rests look very similar. To remember the difference, think of a two-beat rest as light enough to sit **on** a line, while the longer ('heavier') four-beat rest flops down **below** a line.

# SESSION 3

Each time value lasts twice the length of the next shortest time value. This diagram shows how each note length measures up.

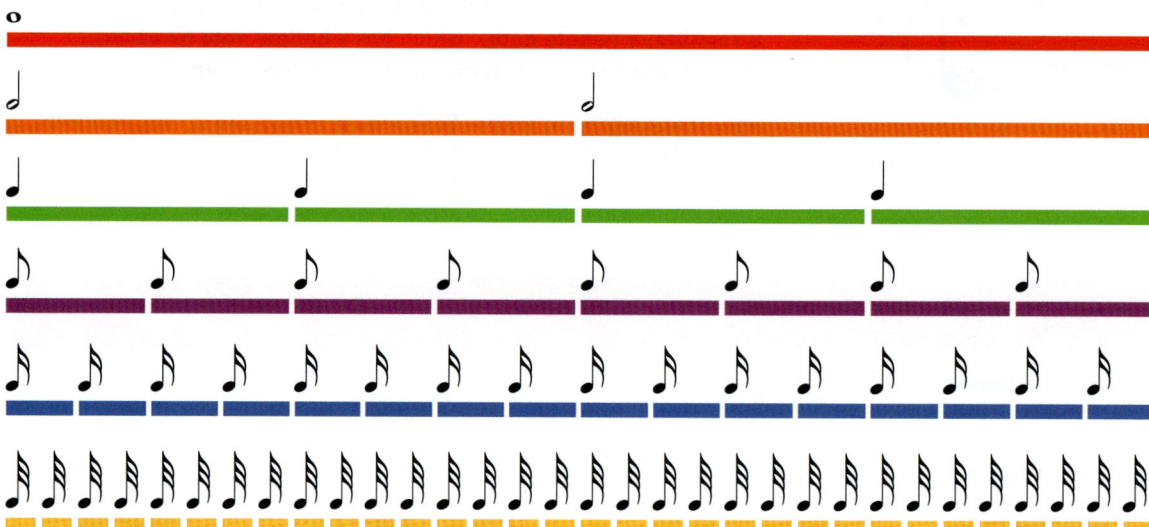

## Dotted notes

A **dotted note** is a note with a dot **after** its note head. The dot makes the note longer by half. Here are the three most common dotted notes:

- 𝅗𝅥 lasts for 2 beats, so 𝅗𝅥. lasts for 3 beats (2 + 1 = 3)
- ♩ lasts for 1 beat, so ♩. lasts for 1 ½ beats (1 + ½ = 1 ½)
- ♪ lasts for ½ beat, so ♪. lasts for ¾ beat (½ + ¼ = ¾)

The dot is always written in a stave space so that it can easily be seen. If the note is on a line its dot goes in the space above the line.

### ACTIVITY 4

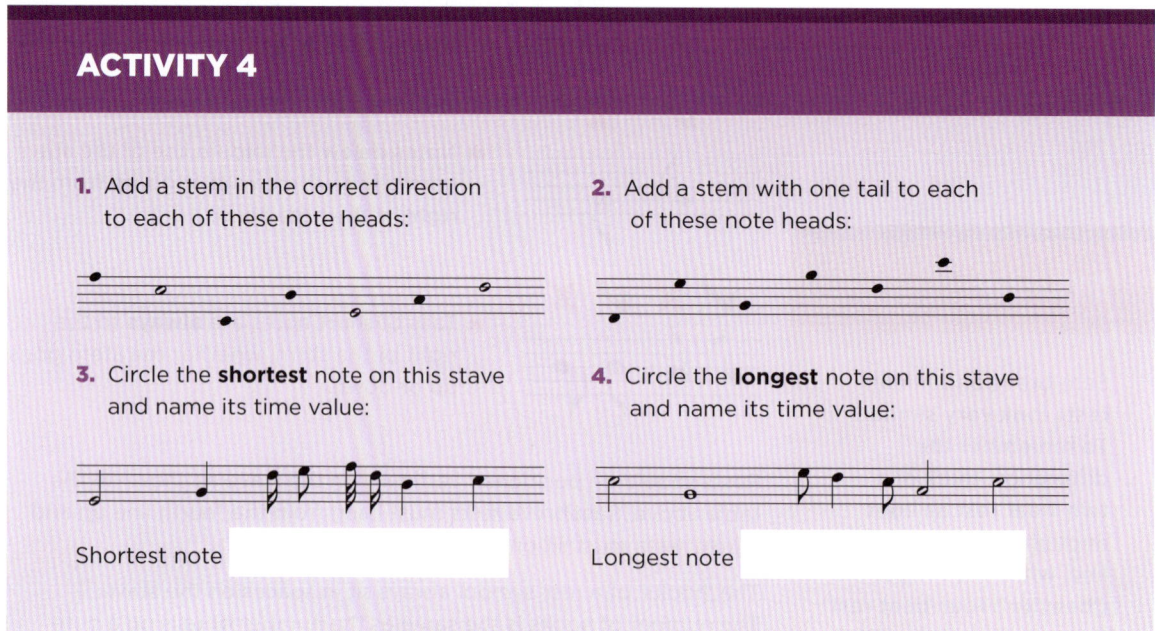

1. Add a stem in the correct direction to each of these note heads:

2. Add a stem with one tail to each of these note heads:

3. Circle the **shortest** note on this stave and name its time value:

Shortest note _____

4. Circle the **longest** note on this stave and name its time value:

Longest note _____

**SESSION 3**

5. Which time value has the same length as four quavers (four eighth notes?)

6. Which time value does *not* have a stem?

7. Which time value has the same length as eight demisemiquavers (eight 32nd notes)?

8. Next to each of these notes, write a rest that has the same time value. The first answer is given.

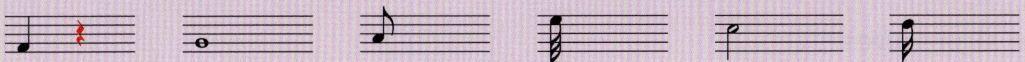

9. Add up the total number of beats in each of these boxes. The first answer is given.

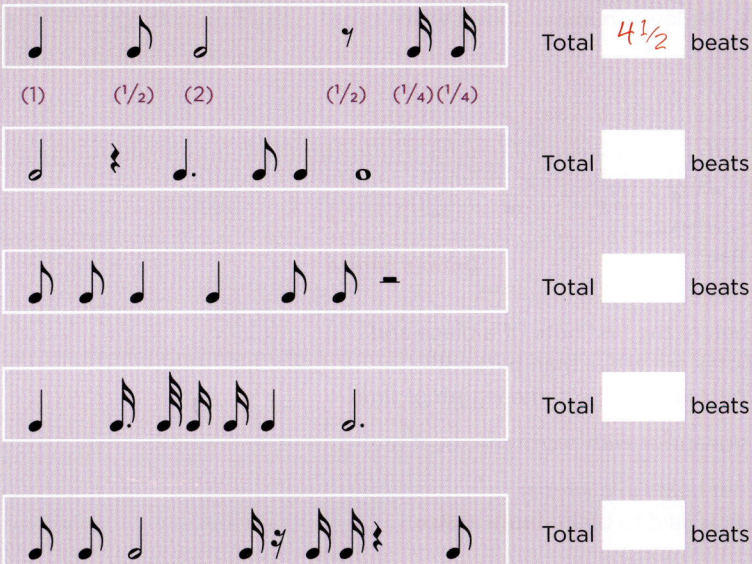

10. Add one or more rests at each place marked ✸ so that the rhythm in each box makes a total of four beats.

A **rhythm** is a pattern of sounds produced by different time values.

## STEP UP

It looks bad for musicians to mis-spell rhythm! The following sentence may help you get it right:
**R**hythm **H**elps **Y**our **T**wo **H**ands **M**ove

## SESSION 3

# Bars and time signatures (1)

## Barlines

Upright lines (|) drawn across the stave are called **barlines**. They divide the music into **bars**, each containing the same number of beats. The first note after a barline is a strong beat, known as a **down beat**. The weak beat before it is known as an **up beat**.

A **double barline** marks the end of a section (‖) or the end of a piece (𝄂).

> **STEP UP**
>
> The terms 'up beat' and 'down beat' come from the movements of a conductor's baton when beating time.

## Time signatures

A **time signature** before the first note of a piece indicates how the pulse (the regular beat in music) is shown. It has two numbers, one above the other. The upper number shows how many beats there are in each bar – typically **2**, **3** or **4**. The lower number shows which type of note represents a beat.

> **3** ← Number of beats
> **4** ← Type of beats

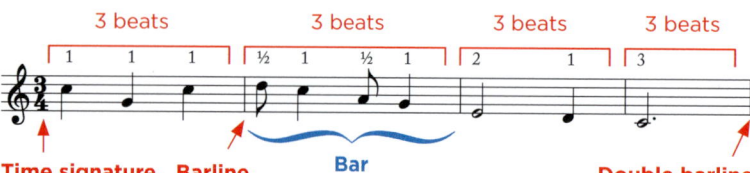

Notice that there is no barline before the first note of a piece and that bars that contain a lot of notes are wider than bars with few notes, even though all the bars last for the same length of time.

The three most common time signatures with a crotchet beat are:

- **2/4**, which indicates two crotchet beats in each bar.
Music that has two beats in a bar is said to be in **duple metre**.
For example:

- **3/4**, which indicates three crotchet beats in each bar.
Music that has three beats in a bar is said to be in **triple metre**.
For example:

> The time signature **C** is often used instead of **4/4**.

- **4/4**, which indicates four crotchet beats in each bar.
Music that has four beats in a bar is said to be in **quadruple metre**.
For example:

### STEP UP

Metre is what you hear or count; a time signature is what you see in the music.

The time signature is only written once, at the start of the piece, unless it changes. It is not a fraction, so there is no line between its numbers. We write 3/4 ✓ not ¾ ✗ and we call this 'three-four time', not 'three-quarters time'.

## Anacrusis

Sometimes music begins before the first strong beat, resulting in an incomplete bar at the start. This is known as an **anacrusis** or **pick-up**. Sometimes the last bar of such a piece is shortened to balance the length of the anacrusis so that the two together add up to a complete bar, as in this example, where 1 ½ beats of anacrusis and 1 ½ beats in the final bar together add up to the 3 beats shown by the time signature:

In the example above, a bar number has been added in bar 5. Bar numbers are a useful way of referring to particular places when discussing or rehearsing music. When there is an anacrusis, bar 1 is always the first **complete** bar.

## The semibreve rest

On page 9 we learnt that a semibreve (whole note) rest lasts for four beats. There are two other things to remember about this rest:

- It is always written in the middle of a bar, **not** on the first beat like a semibreve note.

- It is used to show a totally silent bar in other times, such as 2/4 and 3/4, as well as in 4/4 time, and is therefore sometimes called a **whole bar rest**:

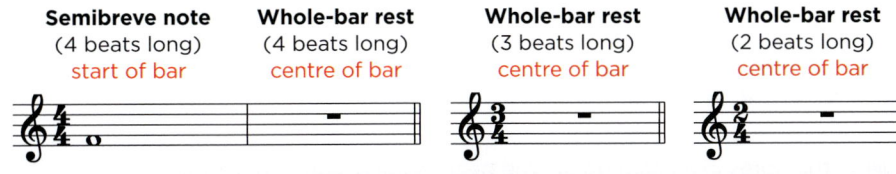

### ACTIVITY 5

Complete the four blanks in the sentences below the music.

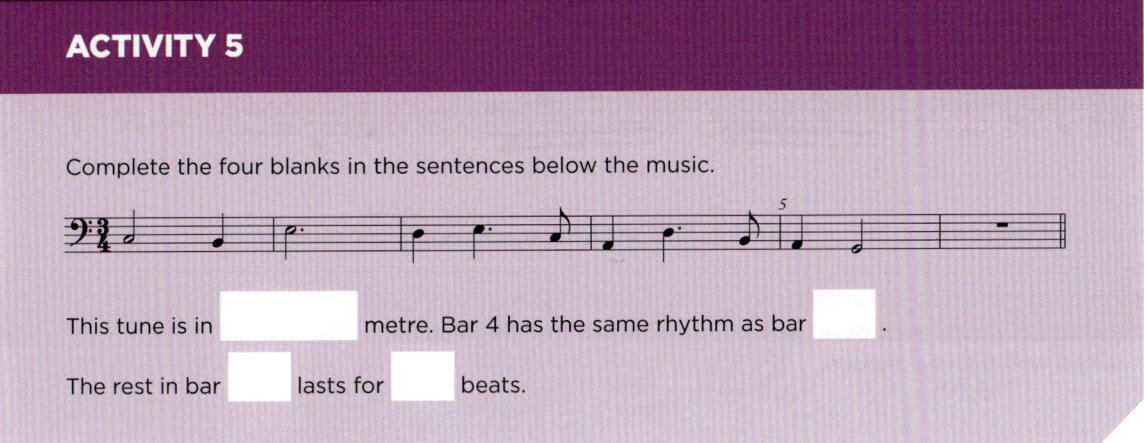

This tune is in ⬜ metre. Bar 4 has the same rhythm as bar ⬜.

The rest in bar ⬜ lasts for ⬜ beats.

# Session 4

## Beaming notes and grouping rests

**To make music easier to read, short notes are grouped into one-beat units whenever possible. This is done by joining them with lines called beams, which replace the tails on individual notes. The number of beams is the same as the number of tails (one for quavers, two for semiquavers and three for demisemiquavers).**

Notes within the same beat are beamed together, but (with a few exceptions given below) notes that lie within different beats are not beamed together. All of the notes with tails in the first row of examples below should be written with beams instead, as shown in the second row of examples. Beats are shown by the red lines below the stave.

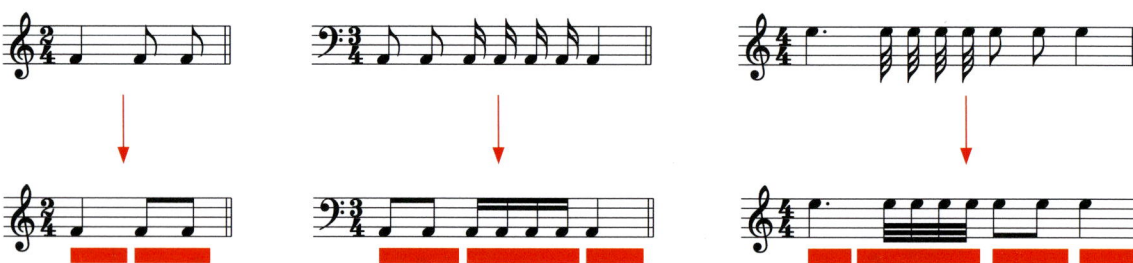

A beam can link notes of different lengths, providing they lie within the same beat.

## Troubleshooting and exceptions

The first beam in the next example is wrong because it links notes that lie within different beats. This example must be written as shown on the right:

When linking notes of different lengths, any short unattached beams should point in, not out.

If all of the notes in a beam go up, the beam should slope up a little. If notes go down, their beams should slope down a little. If the notes go up and down, usually the beam is horizontal.

The stems of notes joined by a beam must all point in the same direction. If most of the notes are above the middle line, all stems should point down, otherwise they should all point up – even if this results in some stems pointing in the wrong direction to normal. In the next example, the stem directions of notes in red have had to be changed so that they can be beamed with their neighbours.

SESSION 4

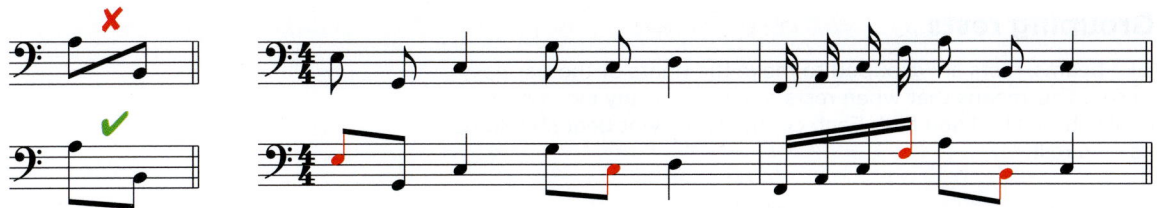

To make long strings of demisemiquavers easier to read, their inner beams may be subdivided into two groups, each worth a quaver, as shown below right:

There are two exceptions to the rule that beamed notes must lie within the same beat:

**Four quavers** (eighth notes) can be beamed together **when they are in the same bar and make up two beats next to each other:**

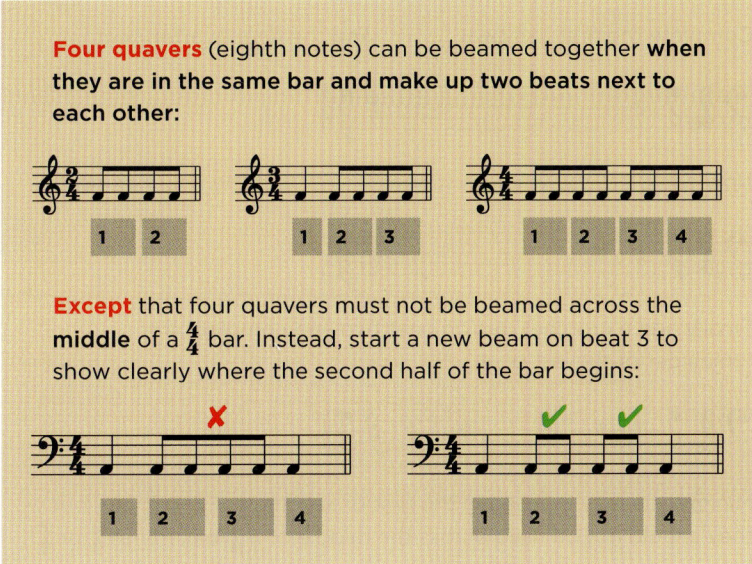

**Except** that four quavers must not be beamed across the **middle** of a $\frac{4}{4}$ bar. Instead, start a new beam on beat 3 to show clearly where the second half of the bar begins:

**Six quavers** (eighth notes) can be beamed together when they fill a whole bar of $\frac{3}{4}$ time:

### STEP UP

To save learning lots of rules, simply remember that whenever possible beams should show clearly the position of each beat. The same applies to the grouping of rests, as explained on the next page.

## SESSION 4

### Grouping rests

Like beams, rests are grouped to make the beats of the bar easy to see. This means that when rests are needed, any incomplete beats should be filled first. Each completely silent beat should have its own rest:

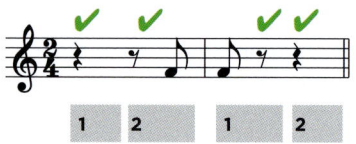 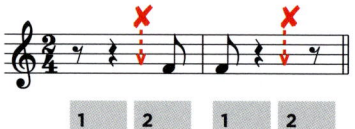 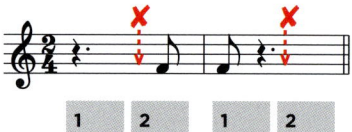

Start of beat 2 shown by rests     The start of beat 2 is unclear when it lies halfway through a rest

When using short time values, begin by completing the subdivisions of the beat with rests, starting with the smallest subdivision. Look at this example:

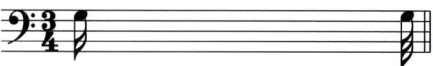

Complete the first half beat ...     ... and the final quarter beat:

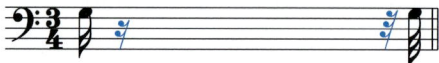

Now complete the whole first beat ...     ... and the final half beat:

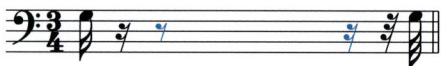

Finally add a crotchet rest on beat two and complete the remainder of the last beat:

Minim rests may be used in the first or second half of a 4/4 bar, but they should not be used across the middle of a 4/4 bar, nor in 2/4 or 3/4 time.

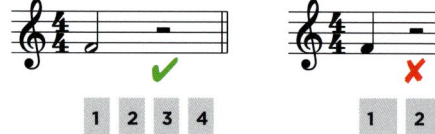 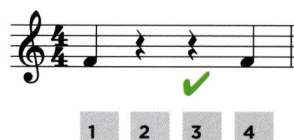

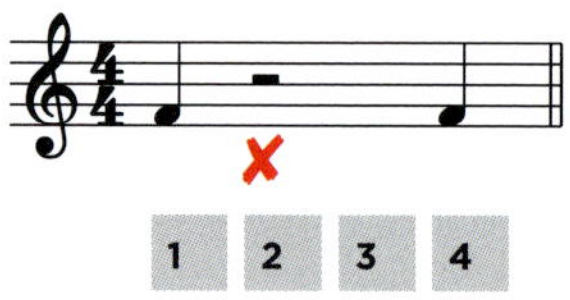

### STEP UP

The rules about minim rests and beaming in quadruple time are similar: the start of the second half of the bar on beat 3 must be obvious.

## ACTIVITY 6

Rewrite this tune with correct beaming and with the rests in the last bar correctly grouped.

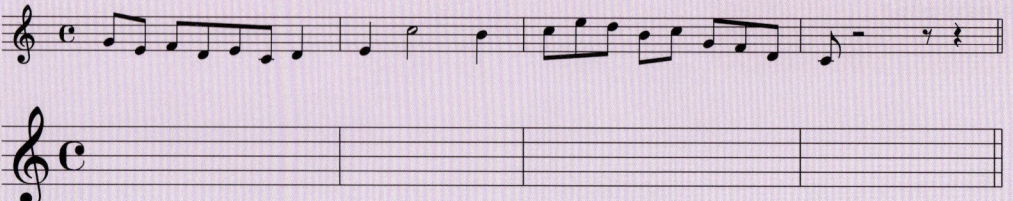

## Triplets

**To divide a crotchet into two equal parts we write two quavers ( ♫ ).**

To divide a crotchet into three equal parts we use a **triplet** (  ). The small figure three just outside the beam is an instruction that these three quavers must fit into the time normally taken by two quavers (or one crotchet).

You can get a feel for the effect of triplets if you say these nonsense words aloud:

**Plinkety-plunkety, hickory-dickory,
Jiggery-pokery, Higgledy-piggledy.**

A triplet of quavers can include rests and dotted notes, and doesn't even need to contain three separate notes, providing its lilting rhythm adds up to one crotchet:

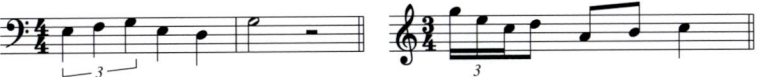

Notice how triplet quavers are beamed in crotchet beats, just like normal quavers. If there is no beam for the figure three (as in the last triplet above) a square bracket is used instead.

Any note value can be split into a triplet pattern. The first example below includes a triplet of crotchets – three crotchets in the time taken by two crotchets (or one minim). The second example includes a semiquaver triplet – three semiquavers in the time taken by two semiquavers (or one quaver).

Other unusual divisions of a note are achieved in a similar way. For example, a quintuplet is shown by the figure five, indicating that five notes must fit into the time normally taken by four of the same value, a sextuplet is shown by the figure six, and so on. These unusual divisions are collectively known as **tuplets**.

## ACTIVITY 7

Make up a verse of nonsense using words with a triplet rhythm.

You could use words of three syllables such as merrily, murmuring, elephants, chattering, tenderly, carefully, Italy, Canada, Latvia, Zambia. If you feel adventurous you might include six-syllable words such as multidimensional, microbiology, hyperelliptical, unsuitability!

You could also include phrases that fit a strong-weak rhythm, such as 'Sounds of music, words of wonder', as these would match a long-short triplet pattern: ( ♩ ♪ ).

# Session 5

## Bars and time signatures (2)

### Simple time

2/4, 3/4 and 4/4 are known as **simple time signatures**. Other simple time signatures have a quaver beat, shown by an 8 as the lower number, or a minim beat, shown by a 2 as the lower number (think of the American note names, shown in brackets on page 9).

The time signature for 2/2 can alternatively be written as ₵ (which musicians often call 'cut C time'). Here is a table of these time signatures for comparison:

|  | ♪ beat | ♩ beat | ♩ beat |
|---|---|---|---|
| Simple duple | 2/8 | 2/4 | 2/2 or ₵ |
| Simple triple | 3/8 | 3/4 | 3/2 |
| Simple quadruple | 4/8 | 4/4 or C | 4/2 |

### Irregular metre

Music is said to be in **irregular metre** if it has a time signature such as 5/4 (five crotchet beats in a bar, grouped as 2+3 or 3+2) or 7/4 (seven crotchet beats in a bar, grouped as 4+3 or 3+4). The famously insistent rhythm in 'Mars, the Bringer of War' from Holst's *The Planets* is in 5/4 time:

### Compound time

When a piece needs a triplet feel throughout, it can be written in **compound time** instead of using triplets. Each beat in compound time is a dotted note that divides into three, in a **strong**-**weak**-**weak** pattern.

The top figure in compound time is always a multiple of three (usually 6, 9 or 12, but not 3 itself). For example, 6/8 indicates six quavers in a bar, in the rhythm **strong**-**weak**-**weak** **strong**-**weak**-**weak**. The two strong beats form duple time and are written as dotted crotchets, as shown below left.

Notice how this differs from 3/4 time, shown below right, which also has six quavers in a bar, but in the rhythm **strong**-**weak**, **strong**-**weak**, **strong**-**weak**.

This music in simple time

... sounds the same as this in compound time ...

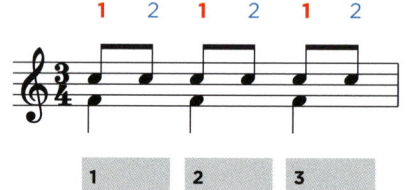

Here are the main compound time signatures, of which the most frequently used is $\frac{6}{8}$.

| | ♪. beat | ♩. beat | 𝅗𝅥. beat |
|---|---|---|---|
| Compound duple | $\frac{6}{16}$ | $\frac{6}{8}$ | $\frac{6}{4}$ |
| Compound triple | $\frac{9}{16}$ | $\frac{9}{8}$ | $\frac{9}{4}$ |
| Compound quadruple | $\frac{12}{16}$ | $\frac{12}{8}$ | $\frac{12}{4}$ |

### STEP UP

Remember, if the upper figure of a time signature is 2, 3 or 4, the music is in simple time.
If the upper figure is 6, 9 or 12, the music is in compound time.

In compound time, short notes are beamed into one-beat groups whenever possible. Beams are never longer than one beat. Remember that the beat is a **dotted** note in compound time – for example, it is a dotted crotchet in $\frac{6}{8}$:

When writing rests in compound time, fill any incomplete beats first, as in simple time. A single rest may be used to cover the first and second of the three divisions of the beat, but separate rests must be used for the second and third divisions:

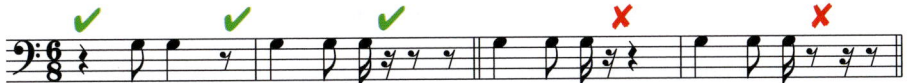

Rests in compound time should show the start of each beat, as in simple time. A silent beat is best indicated by a dotted rest, although two rests in the order long–short are sometimes used instead. Rests longer than a beat are avoided, except that a dotted minim rest can be used in the first or second half of a $\frac{12}{8}$ bar and an undotted whole bar rest should be used for a completely silent bar. The following examples are all correct:

A **duplet** can be used to divide the dotted beat of compound time into two equal halves, or a pair of dotted notes can be used instead:

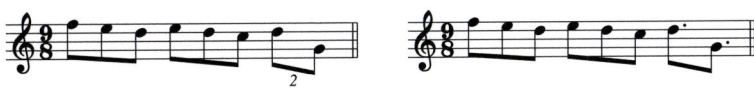

## Free time

Music that has no regular beat is said to be in **free time**. It does not have a time signature and may be marked *senza misura* ('without metre').

## SESSION 5

## Tied notes

**A tie is a curved line that connects note heads of the same pitch. It turns the tied notes into a single sound. Ties should curve away from the note stems:**

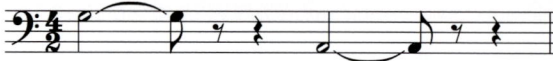

Ties are used for three reasons:

■ When a note needs to be held over a barline and on into the next bar:

1 ½ beats

■ When an unusual note length is needed:

2 ½ beats        3 ½ beats        4 ½ quavers

■ To allow important beats to be seen clearly on the stave, such as the third beat of a 4/4 bar. Bars (a) and (b) below sound the same, but (b) is wrong because it gives no visual indication of where the second half of the bar begins:

Rests are never tied (instead use two or more rests next to each other) and ties are not used where just one note can be used instead. So …

## ACTIVITY 8

Add the missing barlines to the following tunes. The first barline is given for each. Remember that the time signature shows how many beats per bar there are. First, pencil in the time values below the stave, then add ticks at the places that need barlines, as shown for the first tune. Finally, draw the barlines. Don't forget that if there is an anacrusis, the last bar may be shortened to balance.

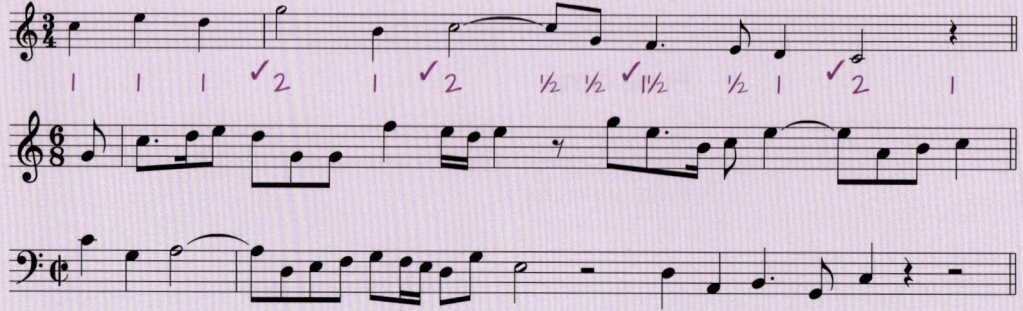

# Session 6

## Tones and semitones

When you play or sing these notes ...

... or these ...

... can you hear that the steps marked ⌐¬, from E to F and from B to C, sound smaller than the other steps?

- A full step, such as the one from C to D, is called a **tone**.
- A half step, such as the one from E to F, is called a **semitone**. Semi means half, so a semitone is half a tone.

It is easy to see the semitones between E and F, and between B and C, on a music keyboard. They are where there is no black note between the white notes:

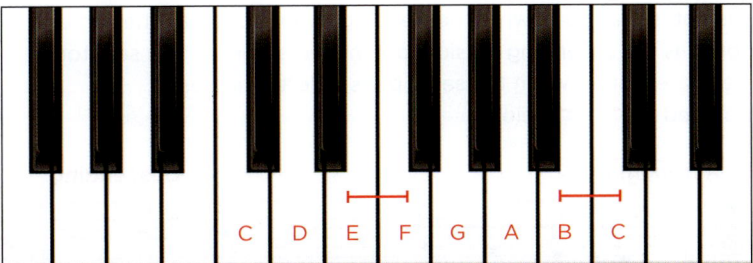

## ACTIVITY 9

1. After each of these notes, write the letter name of the note that is a **tone higher** than the given note.

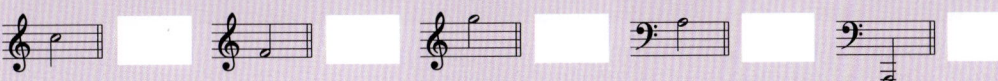

2. After each of these notes, write the letter name of the note that is a **semitone lower** than the given note.

3. Circle each pair of notes in this melody where the notes are next to each other *and* a semitone apart. The first answer is given. You will need to add four more circles.

## SESSION 6

## The scale and key of C major

A **scale** is a set of notes that go up or down in order:

This is a scale of C major. It is called C because it begins and ends on C and it is called major because, when going up, the steps between its notes make the pattern:

**Tone – Tone – Semitone    Tone – Tone – Tone – Semitone**

Every major scale has this pattern when the notes go up. If you learn **T-T-S  T-T-T-S**, you can make any major scale you wish.

Remember these four rules for making a major scale of eight notes:

1. All seven letters of the musical alphabet must be used
2. The first letter is repeated at the end (and is the only repeated letter)
3. A note in a space is always followed by a note on a line, and a note on a line is always followed by a note in a space
4. When going up, the steps must make the pattern **T-T-S  T-T-T-S**.

An **ascending** scale has notes that go up. A **descending** scale has notes that go down. A descending major scale has the same notes as the ascending version, but in reverse order. The semitone steps are still between the same pairs of letter names (marked ⌐─┐ below).

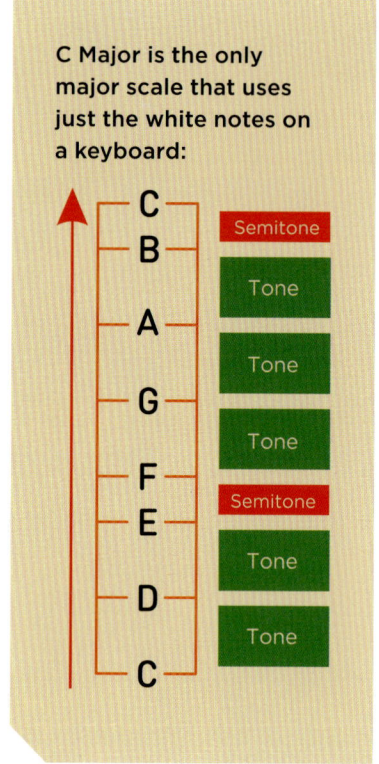

C Major is the only major scale that uses just the white notes on a keyboard:

When music contains mainly notes found in the scale of C major, and C seems to be the most important note, we say that the music is in the **key** of C major and that C is the **keynote**.

### ACTIVITY 10

1. Write an **ascending** scale of C major in the bass clef, starting on the given note. Use minims (half notes).

2. Draw a bracket (⌐────┐) over five notes next to each other in this tune that form part of a descending scale of C major.

*Tahitian Folk Song*

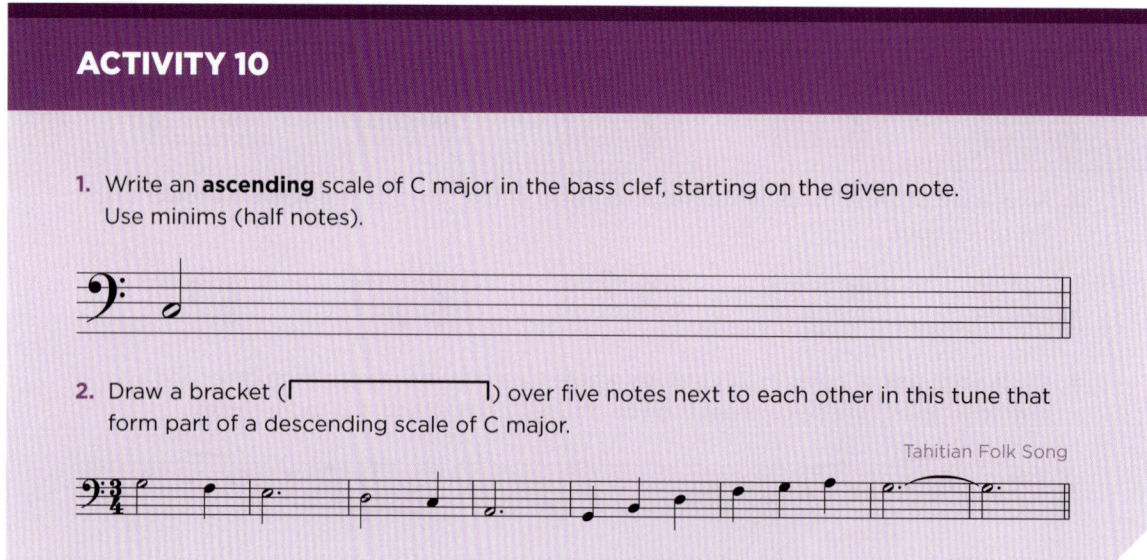

# Session 7

## Degrees of the scale

There are always semitone steps (marked ⌐¬) between the 3rd and 4th degrees of a major scale, and between the 7th and 8th degrees.

The notes of a scale are called **degrees**. Each has a number and a name. When going up, the first note of a scale is the 1st degree, the next note is the 2nd degree, and so on.

The two most important scale degrees are the 1st, which is the keynote (or tonic), and the 5th (the dominant). The mediant lies mid-way between them.

| 1st | 2nd | 3rd | 4th | 5th | 6th | 7th | 8th |
| tonic | supertonic | mediant | subdominant | dominant | submediant | leading note | tonic |

### STEP UP

The 1st degree of a scale can be any tonic, high or low. All the notes shown below are the 1st degree of C major.

When a scale goes down, each note keeps the same degree number and name that it had when going up. The 8th degree always has the same letter name as the 1st degree, and is often described as the 1st degree. However, it is better to think of it as the 8th if you need to count back down from this 'upper tonic' when working out scale degrees, as in the second half of the following tune:

1st  2nd  3rd  1st/8th  6th  5th  3rd

'Sub' means 'below'. The submediant is the same number of degrees below the tonic as the mediant is above. Similarly, the subdominant is the same distance below the tonic as the dominant is above:

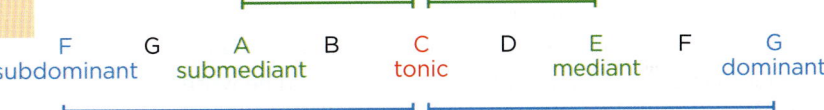

| F | G | A | B | C | D | E | F | G |
| subdominant | submediant | | | tonic | | mediant | | dominant |

The supertonic is the note above the tonic ('super' means 'above'). The leading note seems to want to lead to the upper tonic when the whole scale is played.

## ACTIVITY 11

1. This tune is in C major. Number the scale degree (e.g. 6th) of each note marked ✶.

Beethoven

2. Name the scale degree (e.g. mediant) of each note marked ✶. The key is C major.

Collins & Leigh

## SESSION 7

## Accidentals

**Look at the layout of the keyboard below. There is a black note between C and D. It is a semitone higher than C, and is called C sharp. It will need a sharp sign (♯) in front of the C note head when written on the stave.**

> Remember that we say 'C sharp' and 'B flat', but when we write on a stave, the sign for the accidental goes **before** the note.

The same black note is a semitone lower than D and so can instead be called D flat. It will need a **flat** sign (♭) in front of the note D when written on the stave.

A sharp or flat sign written before a note is called an **accidental**.

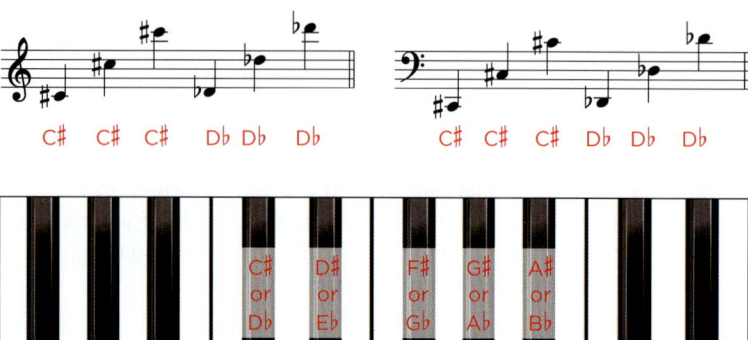

C♯  C♯  C♯  D♭ D♭  D♭     C♯  C♯  C♯  D♭ D♭  D♭

Any of the notes with letter names from A to G can be raised a semitone by adding a sharp, or they can be lowered a semitone by adding a flat.

Notes that sound the same but are written differently, such as C♯ and D♭, are called **enharmonic equivalents**. The note that is a semitone higher than E is normally written as F, but it could be written enharmonically as E♯, while C could be written as B♯. Similarly, E is a semitone lower than F, but it could be written as F♭ while B could be written enharmonically as C♭.

Accidentals must be written on the same line or in the same space as the note to which they apply and they must appear **immediately before** that note:

## ACTIVITY 12

Give the full name (e.g. B flat) of each of these notes.

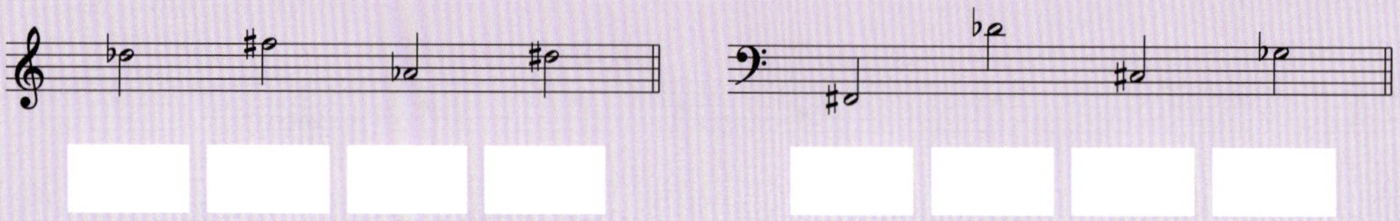

An accidental applies to the note to which it is attached **and** to any note of the **same pitch** later in the **same bar**. In other cases, an accidental must be repeated if it is needed again, except in the case of tied notes.

- The note marked ▲ is F♯, not F, because the sharp on the first note of the bar also applies to the same pitch later in the same bar.

- The note marked ▲ is F♯, not F, because the tie makes it a continuation of the F♯ in bar 1.

- The note marked ▲ is F, not F♯, because it is at a different pitch to the F♯ earlier in the same bar.

- The note marked ▲ is F, not F♯, because it is not in the same bar as the previous F♯.

A **natural** (♮) is an accidental that cancels the effect of a previous sharp or flat:

F natural (F♮) is the same as F, B natural (B♮) is the same as B, and so on.

Like other accidentals, a natural sign must be written immediately in front of the note to which it applies, and on the same line or space, and it too applies to notes of the same pitch that come later in the same bar.

Although much rarer than other accidentals, a double sharp (𝄪) raises a note by a tone (F𝄪 is the same as G). Similarly a double flat (♭♭) lowers a note by a tone.

> **STEP UP**
>
> A 'cautionary accidental' in brackets may be used if there could be doubt about whether a particular note should be sharp, flat or natural.

## ACTIVITY 13

1. Draw a circle around the **lower** note of each pair:

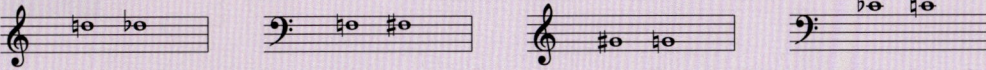

2. Draw a circle around the **higher** note of each pair:

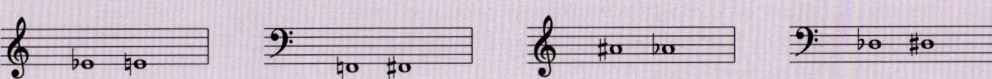

3. Give the full letter name (e.g. A sharp) of each note marked ✱ in this melody:

# Session 8

## Major keys and key signatures

### Key signatures with sharps

On page 22 we learned the pattern **T-T-S  T-T-T-S** for a major scale. The diagram on the right shows what happens if we start the same ladder of tones and semitones on G, the dominant of C. Remember, we already know that there are semitones between B and C, and between E and F.

Can you see that all notes fit the **T-T-S  T-T-T-S** pattern, except for F? To get the correct fit, we need the note that is a semitone **higher** than F, which is F♯. This then gives the correct pattern of tones and semitones for a scale of G major:

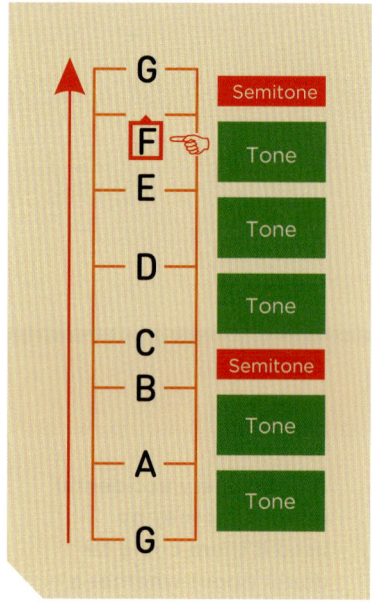

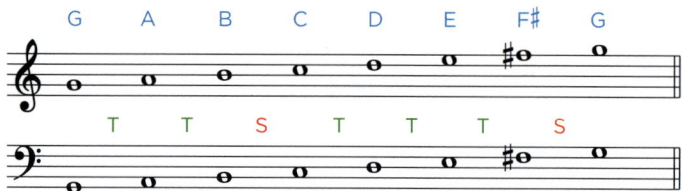

Check for yourself that we have followed all four rules for a major scale listed on page 22.

Music that contains mainly notes found in the scale of G major, and in which G seems to be the most important note, is in the key of G major. To save writing an accidental every time we need F♯ we can use a **key signature**. For G major, this is a sharp sign placed on the stave line for F immediately after the clef, as shown on the right. It tells us that **every** F, however high or low, is to be played as an F♯. Unlike time signatures, a key signature must be repeated on every stave of a piece of music.

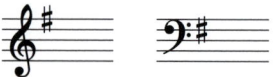

If we repeat the process at the top of the page but start on D, the dominant of G, something similar happens. We retain the F♯ from G major, but the 7th note turns out to be C, which doesn't fit the major scale pattern. It needs to be raised a semitone to C♯ in order to become the leading note of D major. We then have the correct pattern of tones and semitones for a scale of D major:

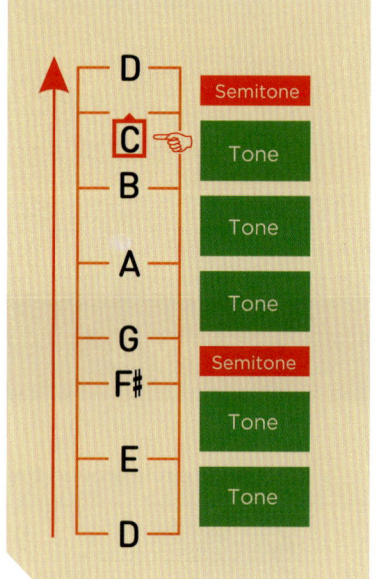

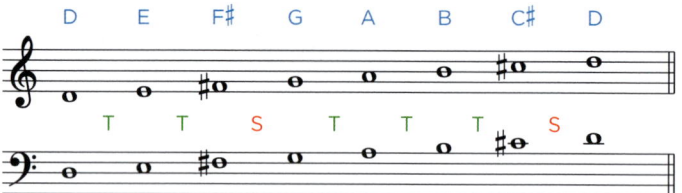

Music that contains mainly notes found in the scale of D major, and in which D seems to be the most important note, is in the key of D major. The key signature of D major is written as shown on the right. The sharp signs indicate that every F and every C must be sharp, unless cancelled by natural signs.

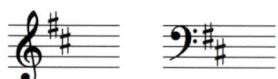

A major scale is simply the notes of a major key laid out in order.

Have you spotted the pattern? When we start a new major scale on the dominant of the previous scale, we keep all the sharps already used and add one extra sharp for the leading note (shown in red below):

| | |
|---|---|
| **C major** | C D E F G A B C |
| **G major** | G A B C D E **F♯** G |
| **D major** | D E F♯ G A B **C♯** D |
| **A major** | A B C♯ D E F♯ **G♯** A |
| **E major** | E F♯ G♯ A B C♯ **D♯** E |
| **B major** | B C♯ D♯ E F♯ G♯ **A♯** B |
| **F♯ major** | F♯ G♯ A♯ B C♯ D♯ **E♯** F♯ |
| **C♯ major** | C♯ D♯ E♯ F♯ G♯ A♯ **B♯** C♯ |

Here are the key signatures for these eight keys. The sharps in a key signature must be written in the order shown, and on these exact lines and spaces.

C major G major D major A major E major B major F# major C# major

0 sharps 1 sharp 2 sharps 3 sharps 4 sharps 5 sharps 6 sharps 7 sharps

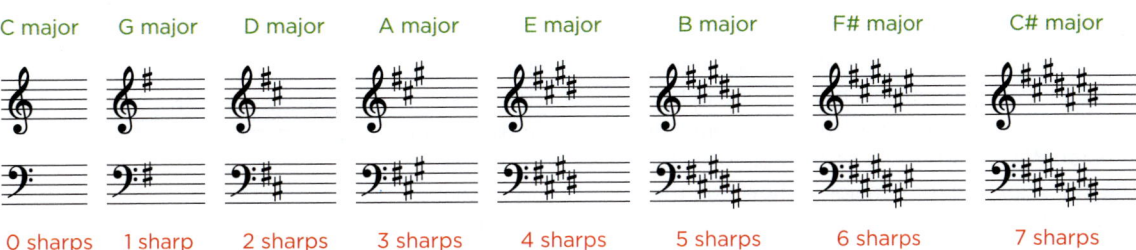

## ACTIVITY 14

1. Give the full name (e.g. F sharp) of each of these notes. Remember to take account of the key signature.

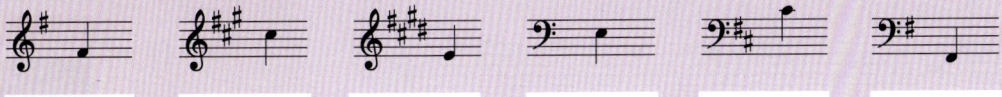

2. Name the key of the tune below: ______. How many times is the dominant used in these bars? ______

   Draw a circle around the leading note.

Traditional English

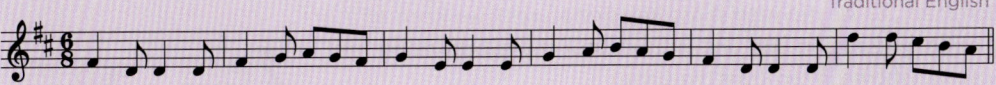

3. Name the key of the tune below: ______. On which degree of the scale does it end? ______

Liszt

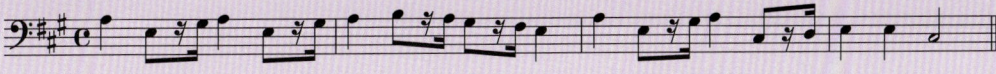

# SESSION 8

## Key signatures with flats

The diagram on the right shows what happens if we start the ladder of tones and semitones for a major scale on F, the subdominant of C. Remember, we already know that there are semitones between B and C, and between E and F.

Can you see that all notes fit the **T-T-S T-T-T-S** pattern, except for B? To get the correct fit, we need a note that is a semitone **lower** than B, which is B♭. This then gives the correct pattern of tones and semitones for a scale of F major:

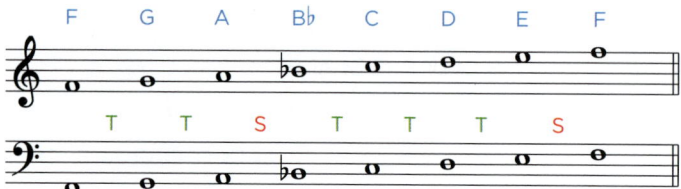

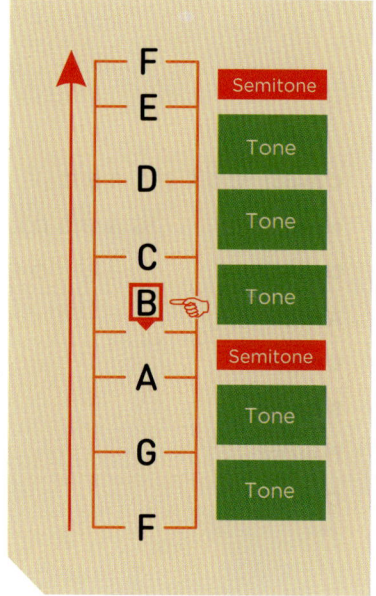

Note that we cannot use A♯ to fit the pattern of tones and semitones, giving the notes F G A A♯ C D E F, because the rules for a major scale listed on page 22 state that all seven letters of the musical alphabet must be used and only the keynote can be repeated. To use all seven letters, B must be changed to B♭, not A♯.

As you will be able to guess, if you are following this chapter closely, music that contains mainly notes found in the scale of F major, and in which F seems to be the most important note, is in the key of F major. We can write key signatures for flats, just as with sharps. The key signature for F major is shown on the right. It tells us that **every** B, however high or low, is to be played as a B♭. Remember, key signatures must be repeated on every stave of the music.

If we now start a scale on B♭, the subdominant of F, the 4th note will be E, as shown on the right. This doesn't fit the pattern of tones and semitones needed for a major scale. E needs to be lowered to E♭ – then we have the correct pattern of notes for a scale of B♭ major:

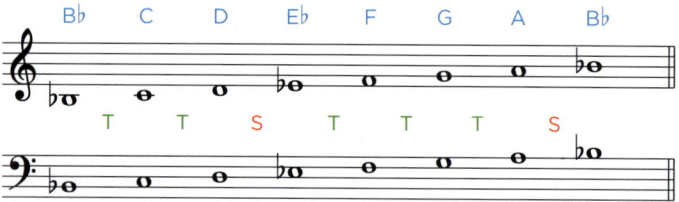

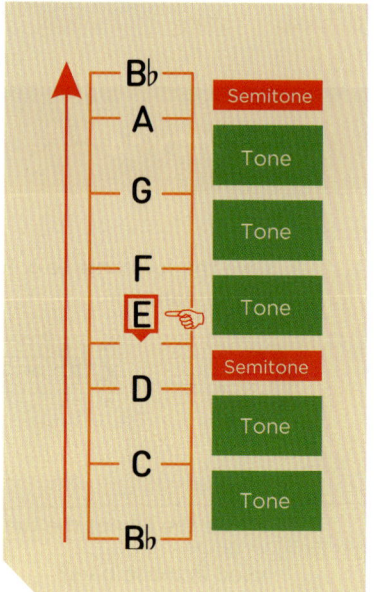

The key signature of B♭ major is written as shown on the bottom right of the page. The flat signs indicate that **every** B and **every** E must be flat, unless cancelled by natural signs.

Have you spotted the pattern for flat key signatures? When we start a new major scale on the subdominant of the previous scale (instead of the dominant, as we did with sharp key signatures), we keep all the flats already used and add one extra flat for the subdominant of the new scale (shown in red over the page).

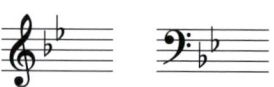

**SESSION 8**

| | |
|---|---|
| **C major** | C D E F G A B C |
| **F major** | F G A B♭ C D E F |
| **B♭ major** | B♭ C D E♭ F G A B♭ |
| **E♭ major** | E♭ F G A♭ B♭ C D E♭ |
| **A♭ major** | A♭ B♭ C D♭ E♭ F G A♭ |
| **D♭ major** | D♭ E♭ F G♭ A♭ B♭ C D♭ |
| **G♭ major** | G♭ A♭ B♭ C♭ D♭ E♭ F G♭ |
| **C♭ major** | C♭ D♭ E♭ F♭ G♭ A♭ B♭ C♭ |

Here are the key signatures for these eight keys. The flats in a key signature must be written in the order shown, and on these exact lines and spaces.

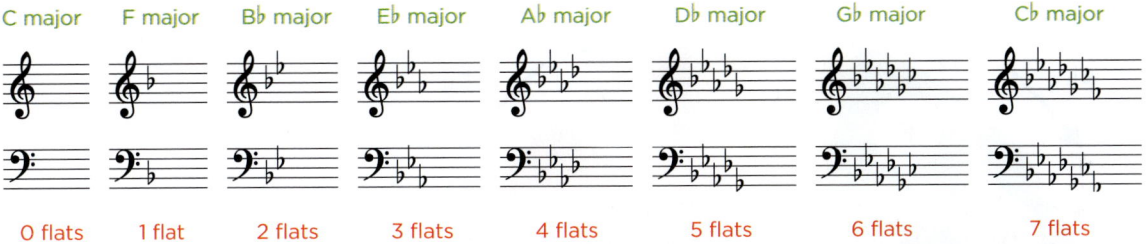

C major — 0 flats
F major — 1 flat
B♭ major — 2 flats
E♭ major — 3 flats
A♭ major — 4 flats
D♭ major — 5 flats
G♭ major — 6 flats
C♭ major — 7 flats

## ACTIVITY 15

1. Give the full name (e.g. G flat) of each of these notes. Remember to take account of the key signature.

2. Name the key of the tune below: _____. Which is the only bar not to contain the tonic? Bar ____

   Draw a circle around the supertonic.

   Con Conrad

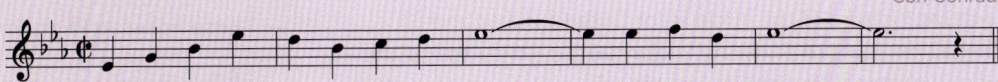

3. Name the key of the tune below: _____. Give the degree number (e.g. 1st) of each note marked ✶.

   Mozart

## SESSION 8

### The circle of fifths

The dominant is the 5th note of a major scale. We describe the distance from the tonic to the dominant as a 5th. For example, C up to G (CDEFG) is a 5th. When you count up these five notes, notice that the lower note counts as '1' (see page 36 for the full section on naming intervals).

Each new sharp added to a key signature is a 5th **higher** than the previous sharp and the name of each new sharp key is a 5th **higher** than the previous key.

Each new flat added to a key signature is a 5th **lower** than the previous flat (for example, the next flat to add after E♭ is A♭ and the name of each new flat key is a 5th **lower** than the previous key).

We can show all of the key signatures in a chart called a **circle of fifths**:

> **STEP UP**
>
> If you find it tricky to count through the musical alphabet in 5ths, remember the sentence **F**ather **C**hristmas **G**oes **D**own **A**n **E**scalator **B**ackwards. The capital letters give the order of sharps in key signatures (FCGDAEB). Reverse this sequence to give the order of flats in a key signature (BEADGCF).

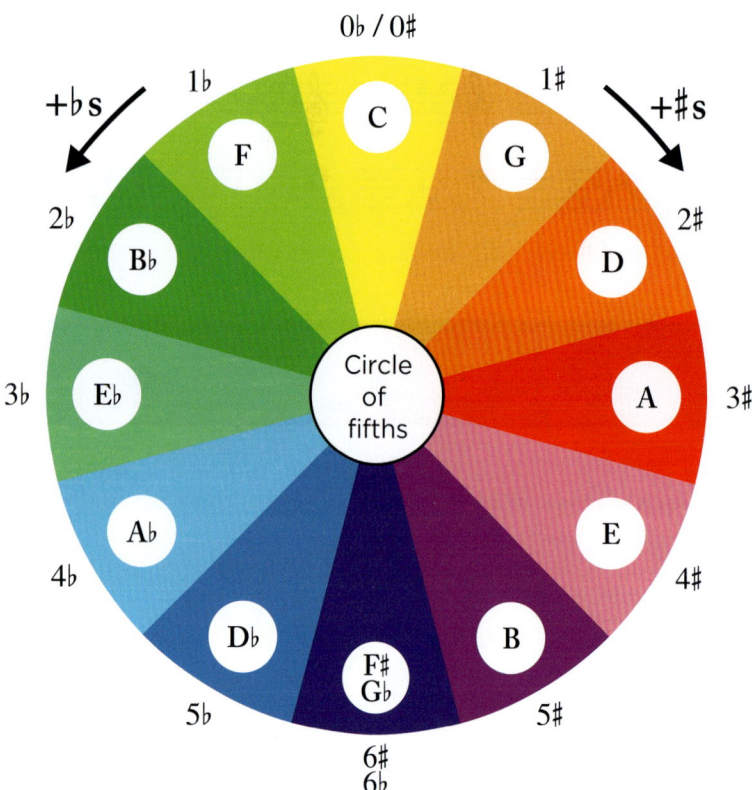

Keys that are next to each other in the circle are said to be **closely related** because they have all but one of their notes in common. The slice at the bottom of the circle is for both F♯ major and G♭ major. These two keys are enharmonically related – they sound the same but are written differently (see right). D♭ major can be written enharmonically as C♯ major (7 sharps), and B major can be written enharmonically as C♭ major (7 flats).

These notes in F♯ major …

… sound the same as these in G♭ major …

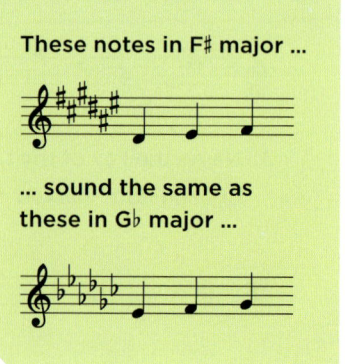

# Session 9

## Minor keys and minor scales

For every major key there is a minor key that has the same key signature. It is called the **relative minor**.

To find the keynote of a relative minor, count two scale steps **down** from the keynote of a major key:

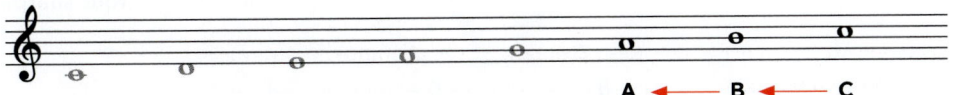

From this we see that:

- A minor is the relative minor of C major
  (and conversely C major is the **relative major** of A minor).

Count down two scale steps from the tonic in F major (F–E–D) to see that:

- D minor is the relative minor of F major
  (and conversely F major is the relative major of D minor).

Count down two scale steps from the tonic in G major (G–F♯–E) to see that:

- E minor is the relative minor of G major
  (and G major is the relative major of E minor).

Let's compare the scales of C major and A minor:

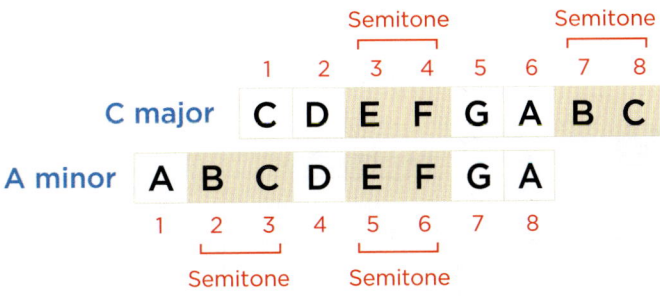

> The type of minor scale shown right is called a natural minor scale. Other types require changes to the 6th and/or 7th degrees, as explained below.

Degree numbers are counted from the new keynote, so A will be the first degree (or tonic) in A minor. In minor scales the semitone steps don't come between the same degree numbers as major scales, and this makes the minor sound different. Some people describe major as sounding happy and minor as sad, although a fast piece in a minor key is likely to sound more angry than sad.

You don't need to learn a new pattern of tones and semitones for minor scales. Just start on the new keynote (A for A minor) and then use the note names of the relative major scale. However, the 6th and 7th degrees of the minor scale are not fixed as they are in major scales. They may be raised a semitone by accidentals, and the raised and natural forms of these notes may be used in close proximity:

The raised 7th degree followed by the tonic is important in confirming a minor **key**. The 7th degree only sounds like a leading note when it is a semitone below the tonic.

## SESSION 9

The table below shows the relative minor of each major key, with its key signature, raised 6th and 7th degrees, and tonic. If either the 6th or 7th degree is already a flat according to the key signature, it becomes a natural when raised a semitone; if it is normally a sharp, it becomes a double sharp when raised a semitone.

> To step up to GCSE music, you will need to know all the key signatures up to and including those that have four sharps or flats.

> **STEP UP**
>
> The tonic in a minor key is always a semitone above its raised 7th degree.

**SESSION 9**

We can add relative minor keys to the circle of fifths. A small 'm' indicates minor. Once again, keys that are next to each other in the circle are regarded as close relatives, while those that are a long way apart are regarded as unrelated.

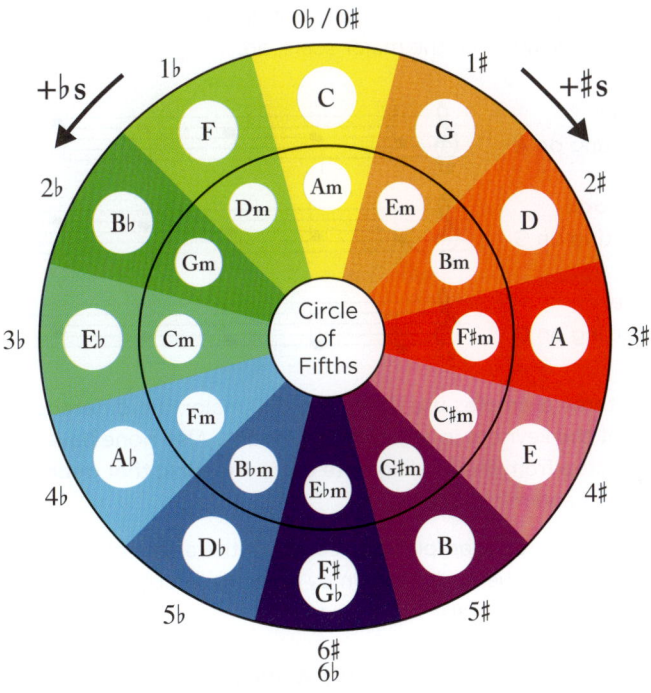

'Parallel keys' are keys that share the same tonic, such as C major and C minor. They are also closely related. When the 6th and 7th degrees of a minor scale are raised, the minor scale differs from its parallel major scale in only one note (E♭ in the case of C minor, whereas C major has E♮). We can say that C minor is the **tonic minor** of C major, and that C major is the **tonic major** of C minor.

## ACTIVITY 16

1. Name (a) the relative minor of A major: ☐ minor, and (b) the tonic minor of A major: ☐ minor.

2. Name (a) the relative major of F minor: ☐ major, and (b) the tonic major of F minor: ☐ major.

3. Name the key of the tune below: ☐. How many times is the tonic heard in these bars? ☐

   Bach

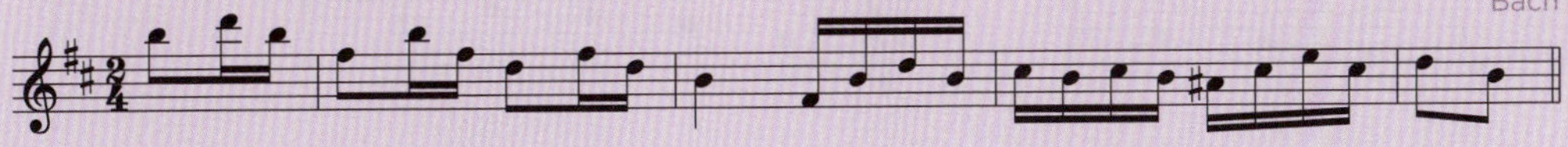

4. Write a scale of D minor **ascending** (going up) starting on the given note. Use semibreves (whole notes) and raise the 6th and 7th degrees by a semitone.

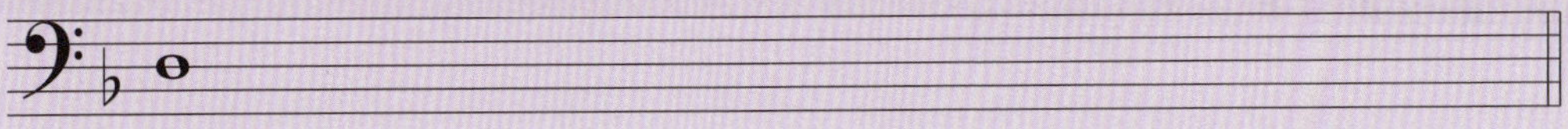

**MINOR KEYS AND MINOR SCALES**

# Session 10

## Modes and other scales

### Modes

The major scale is a type of **mode**. Other modes can be found in folk, rock and jazz, as well as in classical music. The three most common modes, apart from the major scale, are:

**Aeolian mode**
Example starting on A

**Mixolydian mode**
Example starting on G

**Dorian mode**
Example starting on D

Although all three examples use the notes of C major, the difference is that C is not the keynote in any of these modes. Also none have the semitone step from the leading note up to the tonic that defines the key in major and minor scales.

Play or sing these three examples and compare the effect of the leading note rising to the tonic (shown by an arrow) in (i) and (ii), with the modal ending of (iii):

**(i) C major example**  **(ii) A minor example**  **(iii) Aeolian mode example**

Like major and minor scales, a particular mode can start on any note:

**Tune using dorian mode on G**   Brigg Fair (English traditional)

**Tune using aeolian mode on E**   Veni Emmanuel (15th-century French)

## Pentatonic and hexatonic scales

Folk music is often based on 'gapped scales' – major or minor scales, or modes, with fewer than seven notes per octave. A **pentatonic** scale has five notes (just as a pentagram has five sides). Here are the most common forms:

> Playing the black notes on a piano will create a pentatonic scale.

**C major pentatonic**  **A minor pentatonic**

A **hexatonic** scale has six notes (just as a hexagram is a six-pointed star).

**G major hexatonic**

The **blues scale** is a type of hexatonic scale particularly associated with jazz and the blues. The three flat notes below are known as **blue notes**. For expressive effect the flat notes may be played or sung only slightly lower than natural notes:

**Blues scale on C**

The **whole-tone scale** is another type of hexatonic scale. As its name suggests, it contains no semitones between adjacent notes:

## The chromatic scale

A **chromatic scale** contains 12 notes to the octave and is made up entirely of semitones. Using sharps for the ascending scale and flats for the descent keeps the number of accidentals to a minimum.

The word 'chromatic' comes from 'chroma', the Greek word for colour. A chromatic passage adds colour to a key. Music which contains no chromatic notes, and which uses only the notes of the key that it is in, is described as **diatonic**.

## ACTIVITY 17

Using phrases from the list below, describe the scale on which each of the following tunes is based.

**Mixolydian**  **Major pentatonic**  **Whole tone**  **Blues scale**  **Chromatic scale**

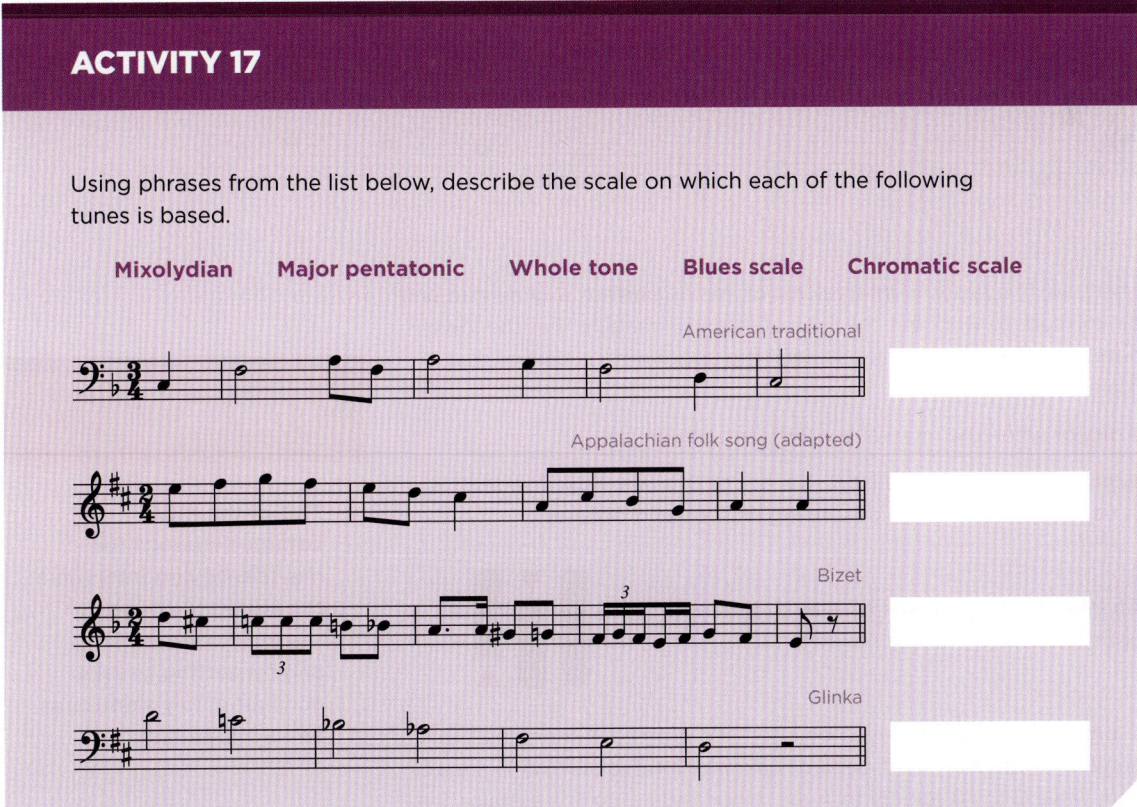

# Session 11

## Intervals

An **interval** is the distance between two pitches. If they sound together they make a **harmonic interval**. If one pitch sounds after the other, they make a **melodic interval**. In this example, all the intervals are the same size because they all have C as their lower note and E as their higher note:

**Harmonic interval**  **Melodic interval**  **Melodic interval**

Intervals are described by type and number. To work out the number, count the letter names from the lower note to the higher note. The lower note is always counted as 1. For example, the interval above is a 3rd (C–D–E).

Each of the following intervals has G as its lower note:

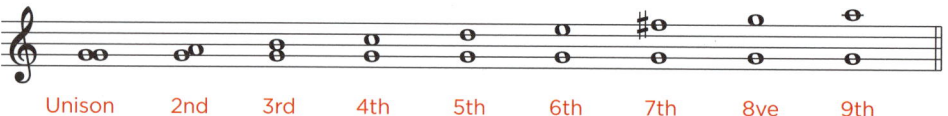

Unison   2nd   3rd   4th   5th   6th   7th   8ve   9th

- An interval of an 8th is normally called an octave (8ve for short).
- Intervals larger than a 9th are often described as 'compound' and then treated as if both notes are in the same octave (see right).
- The notes in harmonic intervals of a unison and a 2nd have to be written side by side, so they are both clear.

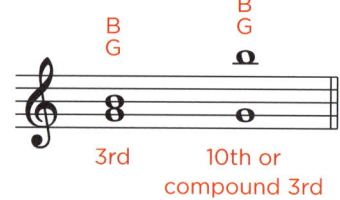

3rd    10th or compound 3rd

The same intervals are found in all major keys. Using the key of F major as an example, here are some intervals that use the tonic as the lower note:

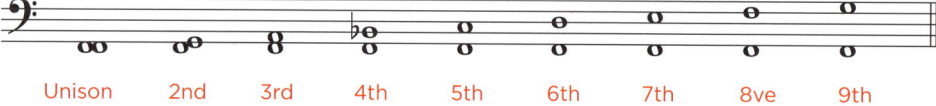

Unison   2nd   3rd   4th   5th   6th   7th   8ve   9th

There are five types of interval: major, minor, perfect, augmented and diminished. To work out the type of interval, imagine that the lower note is the tonic of a major scale. If the upper note is part of that scale, the interval is:

- **major** when the interval is a 2nd, 3rd, 6th or 7th
- **perfect** when it is a unison, 4th, 5th or 8ve (the word 'perfect' is usually omitted when describing unisons and octaves).

An interval can be made smaller by lowering its upper note or by raising its lower note.

### STEP UP

Two of the most common reasons for mis-identifying intervals are failing to count the lower note as 1 and forgetting to take account of key signatures and accidentals.

If a major interval is reduced by a semitone, without changing the number of the interval, it becomes a minor interval. G to A is a major 2nd, while G to A♭ and G♯ to A are minor 2nds; C to E is a major 3rd while C to E♭ and C♯ to E are minor 3rds, and so on.

**SESSION 11**

major 2nd    minor 2nds 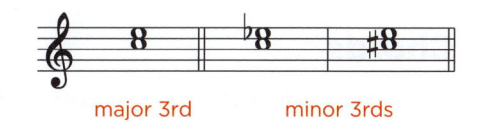         major 3rd    minor 3rds

Minor means 'lesser' when referring to intervals (just as minor roads are of less importance). Minor intervals are a semitone less than major intervals. Minor intervals occur in major keys and major intervals occur in minor keys.

If a minor or perfect interval is reduced by a semitone, without changing the number of the interval, it becomes a diminished interval. C to B is a major 7th, C to B♭ is a minor 7th and C♯ to B♭ is a diminished 7th; D to A is a perfect 5th, while D to A♭ is a diminished 5th, and so on.

major 7th    minor 7th    diminished 7th         perfect 5th    diminished 5th

If a major or perfect interval is increased by a semitone, without changing the number of the interval, it becomes an augmented interval. Thus, C to D is a major 2nd while C to D♯ is an augmented 2nd; D to G is a perfect 4th while D to G♯ is an augmented 4th, and so on. An augmented 4th or diminished 5th (the same interval of three whole tones) is often called a 'tritone' (see box below left).

major 2nd    augmented 2nd         perfect 5th    diminished 5th

Remember: unisons, 4ths, 5ths and octaves are never named as major or minor intervals, as they occur in both types of scale.

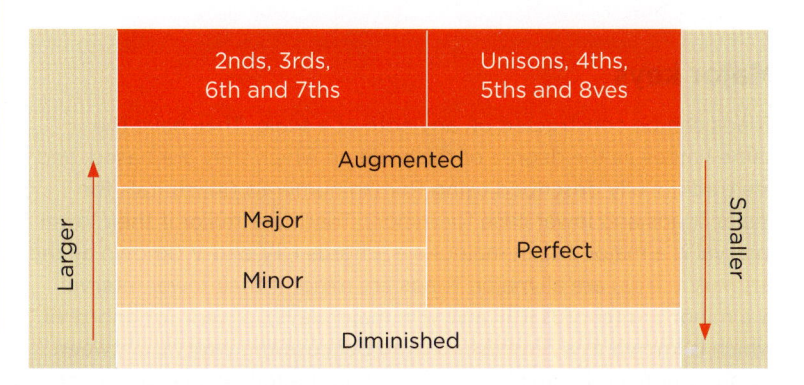

**The intervals below are enharmonic equivalents. They sound the same, but the first is written as an augmented 4th while the second is written as a diminished 5th:**

| | 2nds, 3rds, 6th and 7ths | Unisons, 4ths, 5ths and 8ves |
|---|---|---|
| Larger ↑ | Augmented | |
| | Major | Perfect |
| | Minor | |
| | Diminished | ↓ Smaller |

# ACTIVITY 18

Give the full name and number (e.g. perfect 5th) of each of these intervals:

## Session 12

## Chords

A **chord** is a group of notes sounding together or in very close proximity. Chords make **harmony** – the sounds created when different notes are heard at the same time and seem to fit together.

The most common type of chord is the **triad** – a three-note chord consisting of two intervals of a 3rd placed one on top of the other. For example, a C major triad consists of the notes C, E and G. The three notes in a triad are called (from the bottom up) the **root**, the **third** and the **fifth**.

Above the bass note, the notes of a chord can appear in any order and in any octave; they can be duplicated, and can be sounded separately to make patterns called **broken chords**, **arpeggios** and (more generally) **figuration**. All of the following are examples of a chord of C major in root position, because each one consists of the notes C, E and G, with C (the root) as the lowest note:

> The way in which the notes of a chord are laid out is called the **voicing** of the chord. Sometimes the 5th of a chord may be omitted from the voicing.

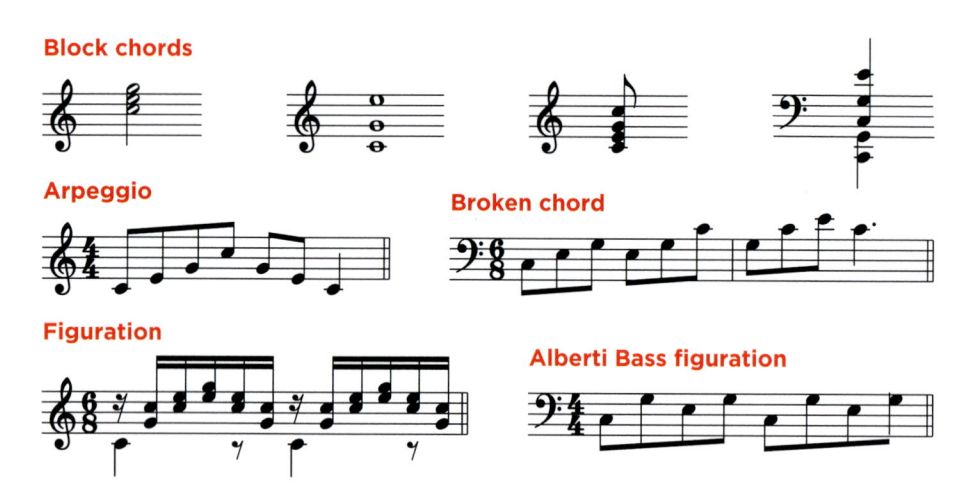

**Block chords**

**Arpeggio**

**Broken chord**

**Figuration**

**Alberti Bass figuration**

## Major keys

Triads can be constructed on any note of a scale. They have the same names as the degree of the scale on which they are based, and are traditionally described using Roman numerals (in capitals for major triads and lower case for minor). Triads are major if their lower interval is a major 3rd. In major keys, chords I, IV and V (known as the **primary triads**) are all major. Triads are minor if their lower interval is a minor 3rd (chords ii, iii and vi in major keys), except for chord vii, which is known as a **diminished triad** because the interval between its outer notes is a diminished 5th (B–F in the following example of triads in the key of C major):

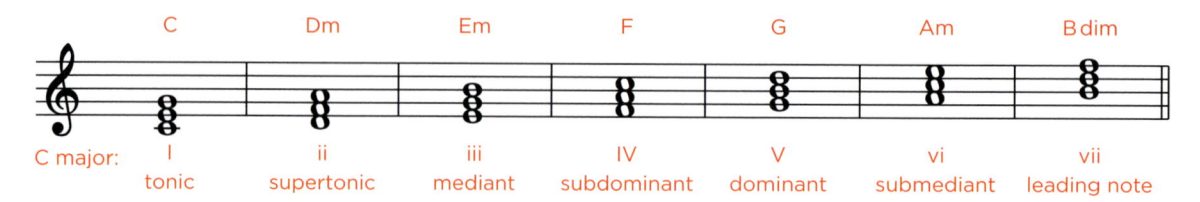

| C major: | C | Dm | Em | F | G | Am | Bdim |
|---|---|---|---|---|---|---|---|
| | I | ii | iii | IV | V | vi | vii |
| | tonic | supertonic | mediant | subdominant | dominant | submediant | leading note |

## Inversions

When the root is sounded as the lowest note (i.e. the bass note) the chord is in **root position**. When the 3rd is the lowest note, it is in **first inversion**. When the fifth is the lowest note, it is in **second inversion**.

**SESSION 12**

**CHORDS**

> **STEP UP**
>
> Non-primary triads in minor keys are more complicated because they can be major, minor, diminished or augmented, depending on whether any 6th or 7th degree of scale they contain is raised by semitone or not.
>
> It is important to realise that major chords occur in minor keys, just as minor chords occur in major keys.

## Naming Chords

There are two widely used methods for naming chords:

- **Roman numerals**: chords are named after the degree of the scale that forms the root of the chord, using upper case for major chords and lower case for minor chords, as in the music example at the foot of page 38. First inversion chords are indicated by a letter 'b', and second inversion chords by a letter 'c' (e.g. Vb or Ic). If Roman numerals are used to describe a chord, the key must also be stated.

- **Chord symbols**: written above the stave, chord symbols show the letter name of the root of each chord. Minor and diminished triads are indicated by adding 'm' or 'dim' after the letter name of the root (e.g. Am or Cdim). If the bass is not the root, a slash followed by the actual bass note is added to the chord symbol (e.g. Cm/E♭ means a triad of C minor with E♭ as its lowest note). This is called a **slash chord**. Chord symbols are often used when notating pop and jazz melodies.

## Minor keys

The primary triads in minor keys are similar to those in major keys, except that chords i and iv are minor triads. Chord V is usually made into a major chord in order to define the key more clearly, which involves raising its middle note, the 7th degree of the scale, by a semitone.

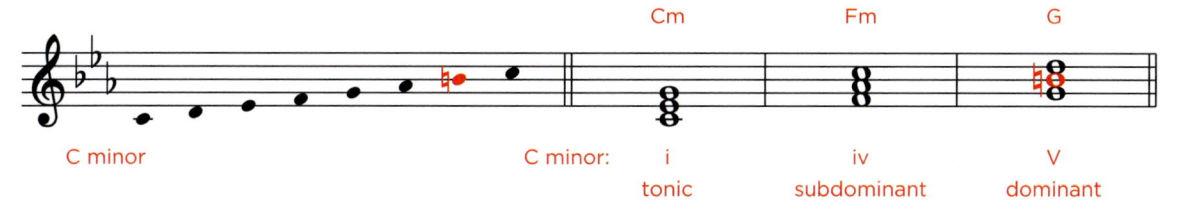

C minor

C minor:  i  iv  V
         tonic  subdominant  dominant

## 7th chords

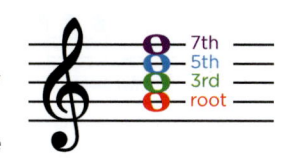

A 7th chord is a four-note chord, created by adding another interval of a 3rd to a triad. This new note is a 7th above the root, hence the name of this type of chord.

The most common 7th chord is the **dominant 7th**, made by adding a 7th above the root of a dominant triad. The **supertonic 7th** (shown below in root position and 3rd inversion) is often used before a dominant chord. The diminished 7th gets its name from the interval between its outer notes:

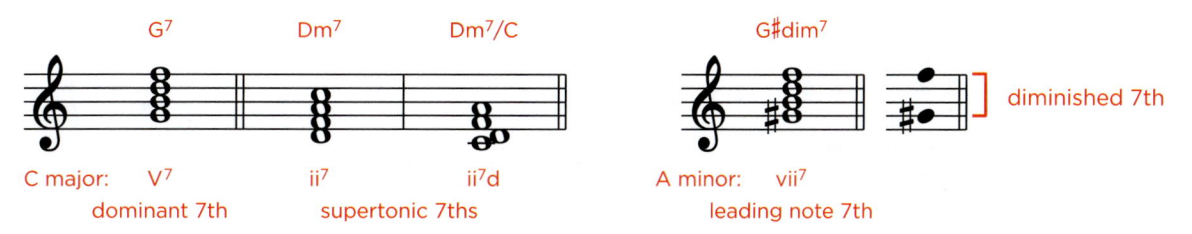

> 7th chords have a root position and three inversions. When using Roman numerals the third inversion (which has the 7th in the bass) is shown by a letter 'd'.

C major:  V⁷              ii⁷           ii⁷d        A minor:  vii⁷
         dominant 7th    supertonic 7ths          leading note 7th

diminished 7th

7th chords are indicated by a figure 7 after the chord symbol or Roman numeral.

## SESSION 12

### Identifying chords

To identify a triad or 7th chord, rewrite it so that its notes are close together on a single stave. To do this you may have to move all the notes into the same octave and ignore any duplicate letter names:

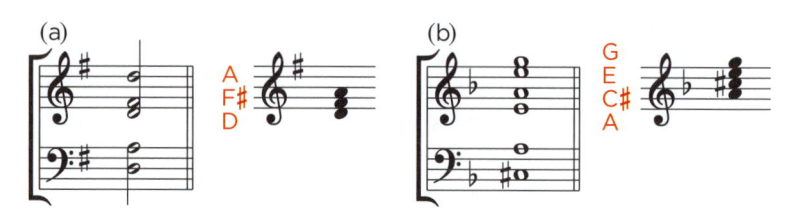

> The notes on bracketed staves sound together.

If the lowest note you have written has the same letter name as the bass note of the chord, as in (a) above, the chord is in root position. This can be labelled with the chord symbol D. Its lower 3rd (D–F♯) is major, so it is a major triad. If Roman numerals are preferred, and the key is known to be G major (rather than E minor), the chord should be labelled as V (because D is the dominant, or 5th degree, of G major).

If the bass note of the chord is not the root, as in example (b) above, show it as a slash chord (A⁷/C♯) or with an inversion letter (D minor: V⁷b).

### Melodic decoration

Music would sound very dull if it consisted of only a string of chords, one to each melody note. Composers make free use of **non-harmony notes** to move between and decorate notes belonging to chords. Look at this example:

Mozart

The chords are actually quite simple – all but one are the primary triads of C major. The real interest is in the tune, which makes extensive use of melodic decoration. Non-harmony notes are shown in red in this copy of the same music:

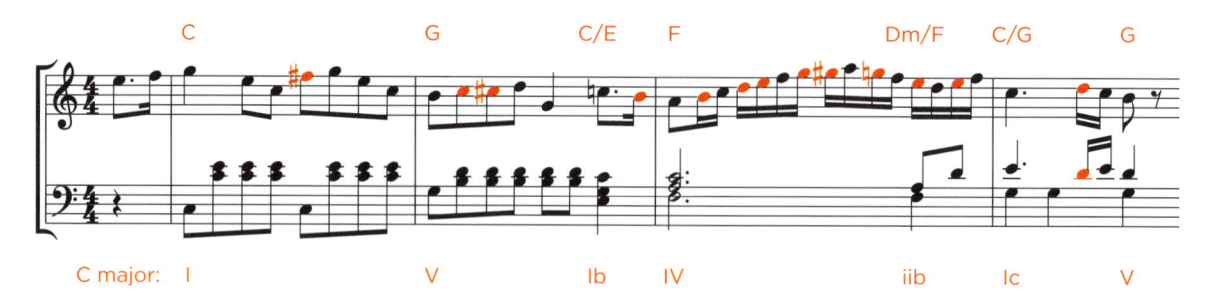

Melodic decoration is ignored when labelling chords with Roman numerals or chord symbols, even when it is chromatic (such as the notes with sharps above).

**SESSION 12**

## ACTIVITY 19

1. State the key of this melody and name the chord on which its first two bars (bracketed) are based.

   Mozart

   Key: ☐

   Chord: ☐

Answer the following questions *either* by writing chord symbols above the staves (including slash chords where needed) *or* by naming the key and writing Roman numerals below the staves (with inversion letters if needed).

2. Label each chord marked ✱ below. As sometimes occurs in music, the 5th is missing from the final chord.

3. Label each chord marked ✱ below. Both exercises are in a minor key, indicated by raised 7th degrees. Several chords on the rest of this page are missing a 5th.

   J. Parry

   Haydn

Notice that chords change on every beat in the first of the two examples above, while they only change once in each bar in the second. The frequency with which chords change is known as the **rate of harmonic change**.

4. These three bars are in the key of A♭ major. Label each chord marked ✱.

   Wagner

## Session 13

## Cadences and chord progressions

A **cadence** is a pair of chords that acts like punctuation, marking the ends of musical statements and sections.

There are four types of cadence, the first two of which also play an important role in establishing what key you are in.

The **imperfect cadence** moves from any chord to the dominant (V), leaving the impression that more is to follow, rather like a comma. The **perfect cadence** moves from a dominant chord to the tonic ($V^{(7)}$–I), creating a sense of completion similar to that of the full stop.

> **STEP UP**
>
> Sometimes, cadences can be suggested by melody alone. Play or sing this example without its accompanying chords.

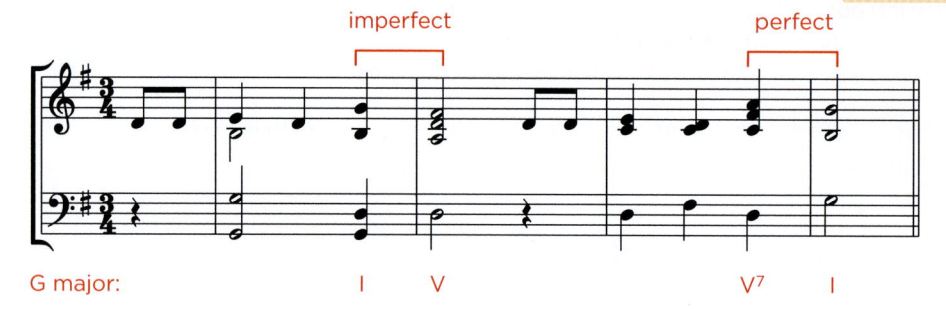

G major:   I   V      $V^7$   I

The other two cadences are far less common. The **plagal cadence** (IV–I) sounds like a sung 'Amen' while the **interrupted cadence** moves from $V^{(7)}$ to any chord except I, sounding as if a perfect cadence has literally been interrupted.

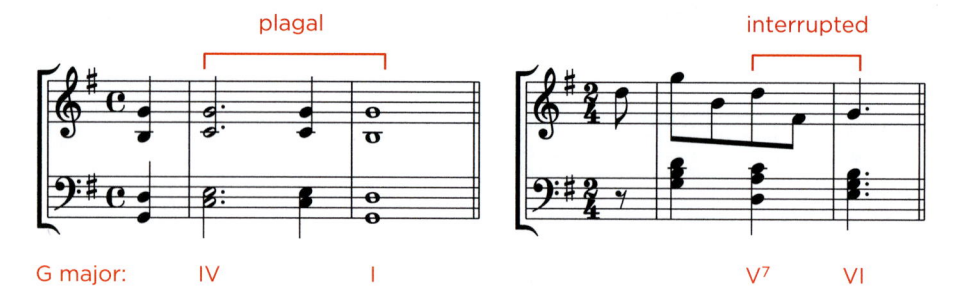

G major:   IV   I         $V^7$   VI

### Chord progressions

A chord progression is a series of chords played in order. A cadence, with or without its **approach chord** (the chord preceding the actual cadence), is a short chord progression. Here are three very common approaches to a perfect cadence, often found at the end of a section or complete piece. The first three are based on ii–V–I progressions, while the last is called a cadential second inversion because its approach chord is a second inversion of the key chord:

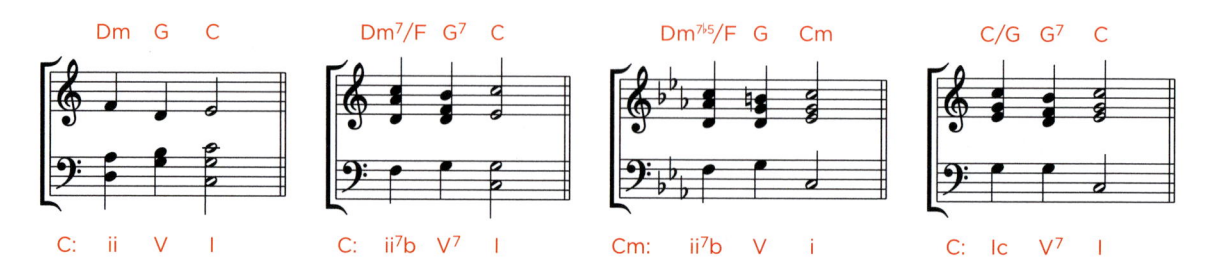

Dm  G  C              $Dm^7$/F  $G^7$  C           $Dm^{7\flat5}$/F  G  Cm          C/G  $G^7$  C

C:  ii  V  I          C:  $ii^7b$  $V^7$  I        Cm:  $ii^7b$  V  i              C:  Ic  $V^7$  I

**SESSION 13**

Most chord progressions are at least several bars in length. One of the most famous is the **falling fifths progression**, in which the root of each new chord is a 5th below the root of the previous chord (e.g. Em, Am, D, G, C). In practice, falling 5ths alternate with rising 4ths (which result in the same letter names) to avoid the bass descending lower and lower.

C   F   Bdim   Em   Am   Dm   G⁷   C

A common variant of this progression is a pattern of falling 3rds, ending with the same falling 5ths as above:

C   Am   F   Dm   G   C

### STEP UP

The falling fifths chord progression is often called a circle of 5ths, even if its chords are all in the same key (with no new accidentals), as in the example on the right.

Another well-known chord progression is the **12-bar blues**, widely used in jazz and rock as well as in the blues. It consists of three four-bar phrases and typically has one chord per bar in the pattern I – I – I – I, IV – IV – I – I, V – IV – I – I, although there are many variants, including adding minor 7ths to any or all of the triads.

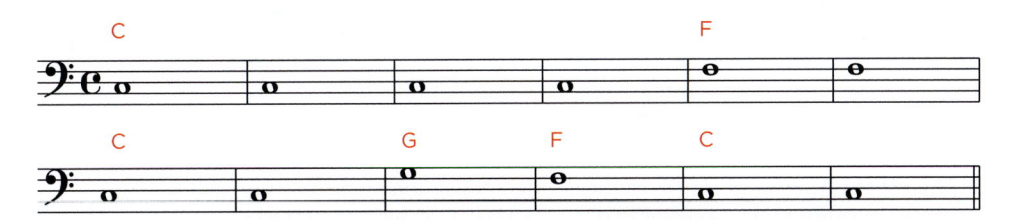

C                                F
C            G      F      C

## ACTIVITY 20

Name the key and the cadence (bracketed) in each of the following.

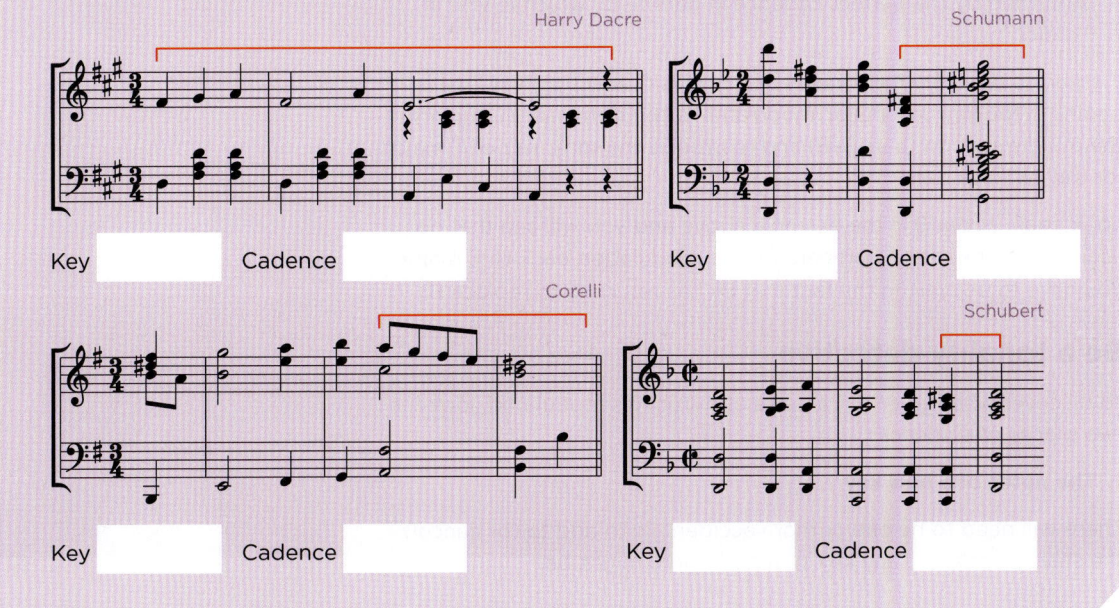

Harry Dacre

Key _____   Cadence _____

Schumann

Key _____   Cadence _____

Corelli

Key _____   Cadence _____

Schubert

Key _____   Cadence _____

# Session 14

## Modulation and tonality

**The process of changing key is called modulation. It is an important way of creating variety in tonal music – that is, music based on major and/or minor keys. Western music that is not in a key or mode is described as atonal ('without tonality').**

In order for a modulation to take place, there normally needs to be a perfect cadence (preferably V$^7$–I) in the new key as well as the correct notes for the new key. Composers rarely change the key signature when they modulate. Instead, they use accidentals to form the notes needed in the new key.

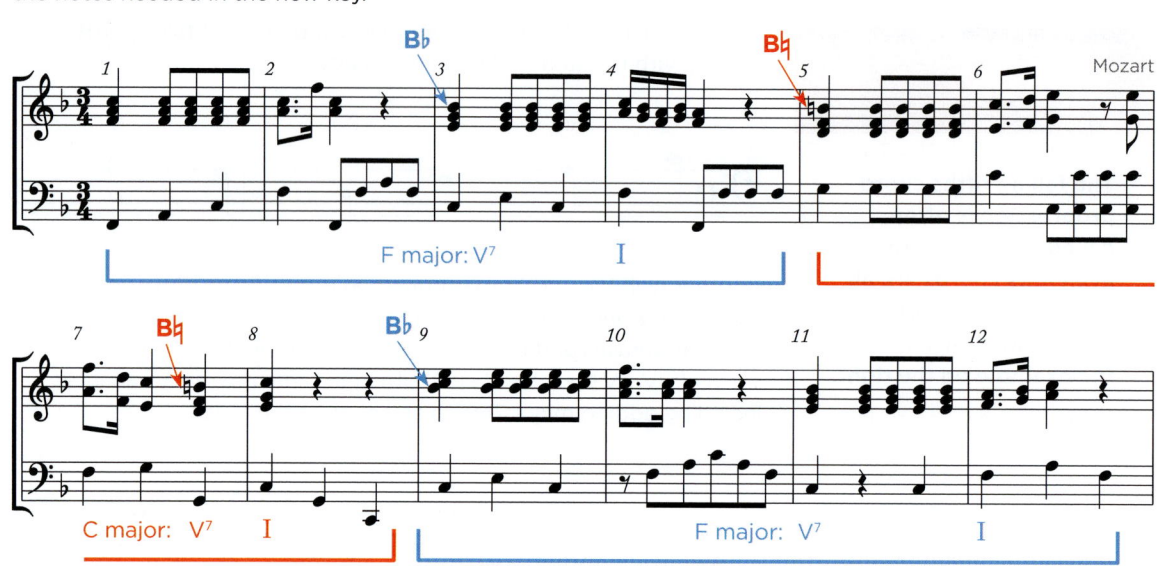

- The piece above begins in F major, suggested by the key signature and confirmed by the perfect cadence in bars 3–4, which is V$^7$–I in F major.

- The B♮s in bars 5 and 7 remove the effect of the B♭ in the key signature. There are now no flats (or sharps) in the music. This suggests the key of C major and this is confirmed by the perfect cadence in bars 7–8, which is V$^7$–I in C major.

- B♭ re-appears in bar 9, suggesting a return to F major. This is confirmed by the perfect cadence in bars 11–12, which is V$^7$–I in F major.

If asked to describe the tonality of this music, we could say that it begins in the key of F major, modulates to the dominant (C major) in the middle section (bars 5–8) and returns to the tonic key of F major for the last four bars.

Look again at bar 9 in the example above and you will see that no accidental is needed to prepare for the modulation back to F major. You have to be alert to the fact that B♭ has returned to replace B♮.

## Be a tonality detective

To discover whether or not a piece of music has modulated, look for two pieces of evidence:

### 1. The notes of a new key

There will need to be one or more accidentals to add to (or cancel) the sharps or flats in any key signature there might be.

## 2. A perfect cadence to confirm that key.

An accidental could just be an innocent chromatic note or an alteration of the 6th or 7th degree if the key is minor. A perfect cadence in the new key is the second piece of evidence needed to confirm modulation. If that cadence ends with a major tonic chord, the new key is major, if it ends with a minor tonic chord, the new key is minor.

A useful rule of thumb is to remember that a note raised by an accidental (a sharp, or a natural that raises an otherwise flat note) could be the leading note of a new key. For example, G# in the key of C might make you suspect a modulation to A minor; E♮ in the key of B♭ might suggest a modulation to F. Look for a cadence in the new key to confirm your suspicion.

Similarly, a note lowered by an accidental (a flat, or a natural that lowers an otherwise sharp note) could be the 4th degree of a new key. For example, B♭ in the key of C might make you suspect a modulation to F, G♮ in the key of A major (3 sharps) might suggest a modulation to D (2 sharps). Again, look for a cadence in the new key for confirmation.

### Case study 1

In bar 1 of this case study, the sharpest note is D#, suggesting the key of E. This is confirmed as E minor by the first perfect cadence.

D# is then cancelled in bar 2 and the sharpest note becomes C# in bar 3, suggesting the key of D. This is confirmed as D major by the perfect cadence in bars 3–4.

Em: Vb    i    D: Vb    I

### Case study 2

In bar 1 here, the sharpest note is F#, suggesting the key of G. The B♭ in the key signature may lead to the expectation that the key is G minor, but the B♮ in the tonic chord of the first perfect cadence confirms the key of G major. The B♮ is replaced by B♭ in bar 3.

There are no other accidentals, so we have the notes of F major, confirmed by the perfect cadence in bars 3–4. The notes in bars 2 and 4 shown in grey are non-harmony notes.

G: Vb    I    F: Vb    I

When music stays in a new key for only a very short period (as in both examples above) we often say that the music 'passes through' the keys concerned.

Modulations are often to closely related keys, as shown in the circle of 5ths (on page 33). In simple pieces modulations are likely to be from a major key to its dominant and back, or from a minor key to its relative major and back.

# SESSION 14

Accidentals do not always indicate modulation, they could simply be chromatic decoration. In the following example, C♯ might suggest D minor and B♮ might suggest C major, but the perfect cadence is in F major: there is no modulation.

The notes with arrows are purely chromatic decoration.

*Beethoven*

F:   V        I

Perfect cadences in minor keys sometimes end on a **major** tonic chord (e.g. a chord of A major in the key of A minor, as shown left). This is not in itself a modulation but this effect of a raised 3rd in the tonic chord is called a **Tierce de Picardie**.

## ACTIVITY 21

1. Look at these four bars and then complete the sentences below:

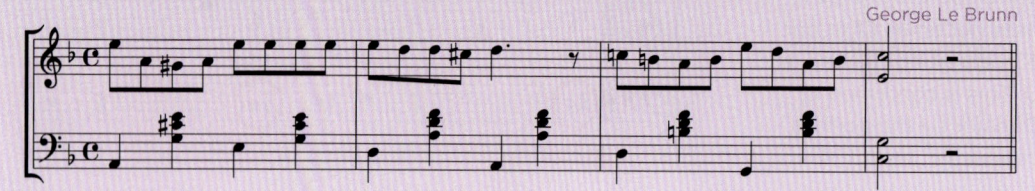

*George Le Brunn*

The V⁷-I progression in bars 1–2 is in the key of: _____, while the V⁷-I progression in bars 3–4 is in the key of _____. The letter name of the only chromatic note in these four bars is _____.

2. Name the key in which the following passage starts and the key in which it ends:

*Schubert*

Starting key: _____    Ending key: _____

3. This extract begins in G major. To which key does it modulate in the last two bars?

_____

*Rossini*

# Knowledge

Note that some Italian words are very similar to English, such as **moderato** (moderately) and **espressivo** (expressively).

## Terms and signs

In the early days of music printing, many of the most famous composers came from Italy. Musicians in other countries became used to seeing instructions on how to play a piece in Italian, and we still use many of these words today. Some of the more common Italian terms are listed below.

### Tempo directions

**Tempo** means 'time' and refers to the speed at which music is played or sung. Most pieces have a tempo direction at the start of the music, printed above the time signature. It tells you how fast or slow to perform the music. A fast tempo means a fast speed and a slow tempo means a slow speed.

| | | | |
|---|---|---|---|
| **lento** | very slow | **moderato** | moderately |
| **adagio** | slow | **allegro moderato** | moderately fast |
| **largo** | broadly (quite slow) | **allegro** | fast, joyful |
| **andante** | walking pace (not too slow) | **vivace** | lively |
| **allegretto** | a little brisk | **presto** | very quick |

*A clockwork metronome*

Tempo can be indicated more exactly by the number of beats in a minute. All of the following mean 60 crotchet beats per minute – one beat per second – which is a slow speed:

**60 bpm** — bpm stands for beats per minute
♩=60 — the number of crotchet (quarter note) beats per minute
**M.M.** ♩=60 — M.M. is short for Maelzel's Metronome (see left)

The metronome, invented 200 years ago by Johann Maelzel, can be set to click the speed of the beat. If you don't own a traditional clockwork or electronic model, there are several free metronome websites and plenty of apps available.

The higher the number, the faster the speed. For instance 120 bpm or ♩=120 means 120 beats a minute, two beats per second, which is a fast speed.

*An electronic metronome*

### Tempo change

Directions used if the tempo should be modified or the beat interrupted:

| | |
|---|---|
| **accelerando** (or **accel.**) | gradually speed up |
| **rallentando** (or **rall.**) | gradually slow down |
| **ritardando** (**ritard.** or **rit.**) | gradually slow down |
| **allargando** | get slower and broader |
| **ritenuto** (**riten.** or **rit.**) | hold back, immediately slower |
| **a tempo** | 'in time': return to the original speed after a change of speed |
| **rubato** | literally 'robbed time': play the rhythm freely for expressive effect |
| 𝄐 | a pause sign (or 'fermata') indicates that a note or rest should be held for longer than normal |
|  (music notation example) | a caesura (//) or a breath mark (,) above the stave indicates a brief silence |

## Dynamics

A **dynamic** marking indicates how loud or soft music should be. Usually dynamics are shown by the abbreviations or signs listed below, rather than by full words.

| Abbreviation or sign | Full word | Meaning |
|---|---|---|
| *pp* | pianissimo | very soft |
| *p* | piano | soft |
| *mp* | mezzo-piano | medium soft ⎫ *mezzo* is Italian for |
| *mf* | mezzo-forte | medium loud ⎭ 'half' or 'medium' |
| *f* | forte | loud |
| *ff* | fortissimo | very loud |
| *fp* | fortepiano | loud, then immediately soft |
| &lt;  or *cresc.* | crescendo | gradually get louder |
| &gt;  or *dim.* | diminuendo | gradually get softer |

## Expression

| | | | |
|---|---|---|---|
| affettuoso | with feeling, tenderly | leggiero | lightly |
| appassionato | passionately | maestoso | majestically |
| agitato | agitated | marcato | marked, accented |
| animato | animated, lively | marziale | in a march style |
| cantabile | in a singing style | pesante | heavily |
| con forza | with force | risoluto | boldly |
| delicato | delicately | ritmico | rhythmically |
| dolce | sweetly | scherzando | playfully, merrily |
| espressivo | expressively | simile (sim.) | (continue) similarly |
| giocoso | playfully | sostenuto | sustained |
| grazioso | gracefully | staccato (stacc.) | detached (see page 49) |
| legato | smoothly | tranquillo | calmly |

## Qualifying words

| Italian term | Meaning | Example |
|---|---|---|
| al, alla | in the style of | **alla marcia** (in the style of a march) |
| assai | very | **presto assai** (very quick) |
| col, con | with | **con moto** (with movement) |
| e, ed | and | **piano e staccato** (soft and detached) |
| ma | but | **allegro ma non troppo** (fast, but not too much so) |
| meno | less | **meno mosso** (less movement, slower) |
| molto | much, very | **molto adagio** (very slowly) |
| più | more | **più forte** (more loudly) |
| poco a poco | little by little | **poco a poco cresc.** (get louder little by little) |
| quasi | as if | **quasi corni** (resembling [the sound of] horns) |
| sempre | always | **sempre legato** (always smoothly) |
| subito | suddenly | **attacca subito** (begin [the next part] immediately) |

## Articulation marks

**Articulation marks** indicate how individual notes (or groups of notes) should be performed. They are normally written above or below a note head, on the opposite side to the stem.

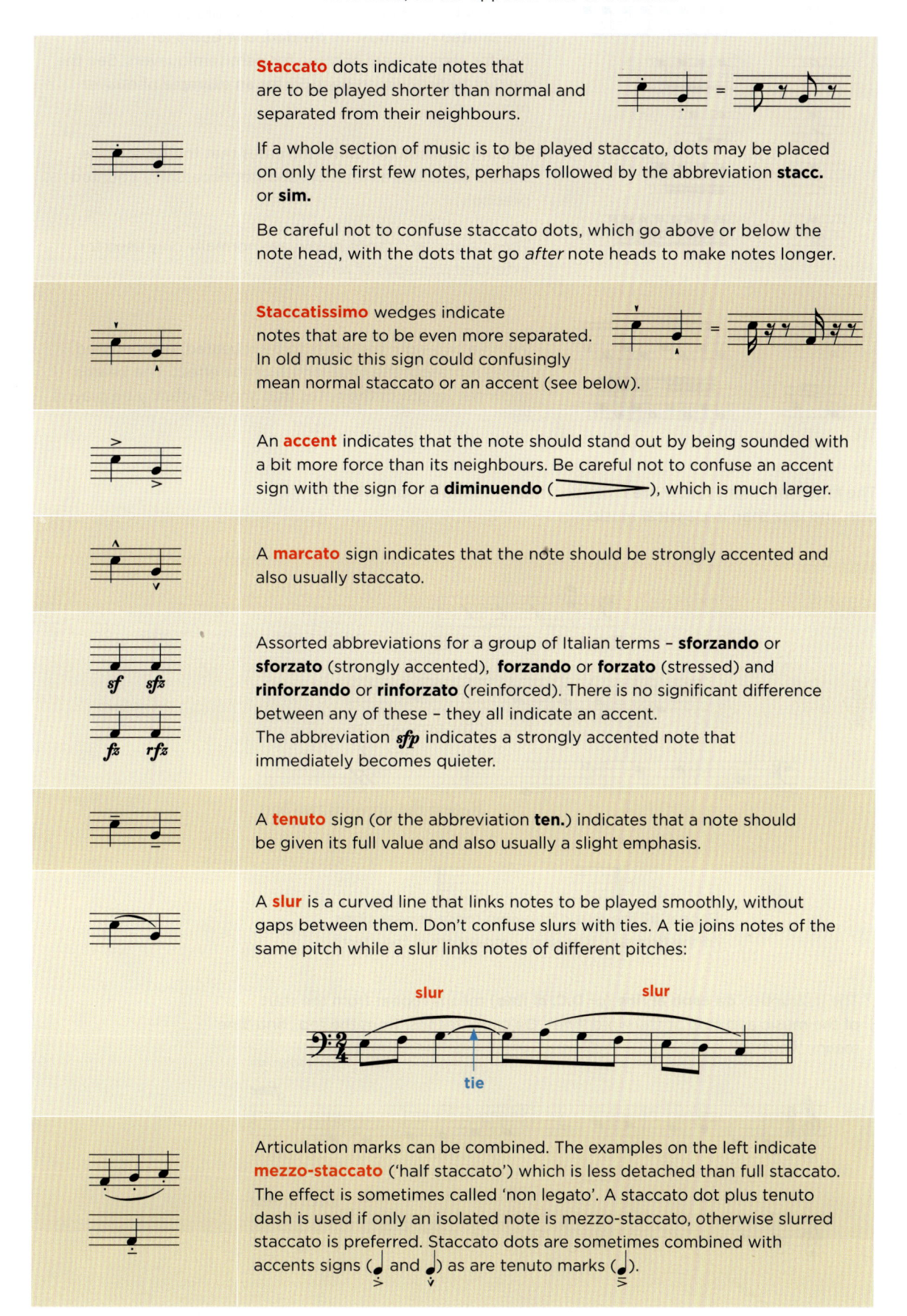

**Staccato** dots indicate notes that are to be played shorter than normal and separated from their neighbours.

If a whole section of music is to be played staccato, dots may be placed on only the first few notes, perhaps followed by the abbreviation **stacc.** or **sim.**

Be careful not to confuse staccato dots, which go above or below the note head, with the dots that go *after* note heads to make notes longer.

**Staccatissimo** wedges indicate notes that are to be even more separated. In old music this sign could confusingly mean normal staccato or an accent (see below).

An **accent** indicates that the note should stand out by being sounded with a bit more force than its neighbours. Be careful not to confuse an accent sign with the sign for a **diminuendo** ( ), which is much larger.

A **marcato** sign indicates that the note should be strongly accented and also usually staccato.

Assorted abbreviations for a group of Italian terms – **sforzando** or **sforzato** (strongly accented), **forzando** or **forzato** (stressed) and **rinforzando** or **rinforzato** (reinforced). There is no significant difference between any of these – they all indicate an accent.
The abbreviation *sfp* indicates a strongly accented note that immediately becomes quieter.

A **tenuto** sign (or the abbreviation **ten.**) indicates that a note should be given its full value and also usually a slight emphasis.

A **slur** is a curved line that links notes to be played smoothly, without gaps between them. Don't confuse slurs with ties. A tie joins notes of the same pitch while a slur links notes of different pitches:

Articulation marks can be combined. The examples on the left indicate **mezzo-staccato** ('half staccato') which is less detached than full staccato. The effect is sometimes called 'non legato'. A staccato dot plus tenuto dash is used if only an isolated note is mezzo-staccato, otherwise slurred staccato is preferred. Staccato dots are sometimes combined with accents signs ( and ) as are tenuto marks ( ).

# KNOWLEDGE

## Signs for repetition

| Example | Played as | Explanation |
|---|---|---|
| | | The number of beams shows the type of note into which the printed note must be divided: one beam for quavers, two for semiquavers or three for demisemiquavers. See the extract by Sullivan on page 59 for an example of quaver repetition.<br><br>Adding **tremolo** (or **trem.**) indicates that the repetitions should be as fast as possible and not necessarily counted precisely.<br><br>These signs, and those below, are normally only used for extended passages of repetition. |
| | | When a two-note pattern is to be repeated, both printed notes represent the total length of the effect. The beams show the length of the notes that should actually be played. |

The first three signs below are more commonly found in scores of pop and jazz than in classical music.

Repeat the previous beat

Repeat the previous bar

Repeat the previous two bars

Repeat all the music between these repeat signs
(if the first sign is missing, repeat from the start)

The instruction **da capo al fine** (or **D.C. al fine**) means repeat from the start of the music and stop at the word 'fine'. 'Da capo' means 'from the top', and 'fine' means 'finish':

Traditional

*fine*

end here

repeat from the start

*D.C. al fine*

# KNOWLEDGE

**TERMS AND SIGNS**

If the instruction is **dal segno** (or **D.S.**), meaning 'from the sign', the repeat is not from the start of the music, but from a place marked by a sign (usually 𝄋).

After a repeat there may be an instruction, particularly in pop songs, to jump forward to a final section called a **coda**, in the form **D.C. al coda** or **D.S. al coda**. The start of a coda is usually marked ⊕.

When a repeat needs a different ending, first- and second-time bars are used. In this example, the bars marked |1.         | are replaced by the bar marked |2.        | when the music is repeated:

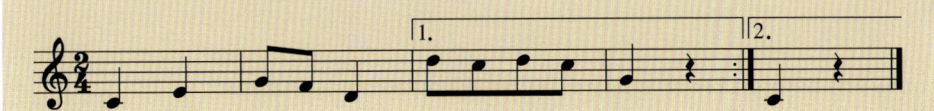

The **multi-bar rest** is used in music for individual instruments when a player has a long rest (46 bars in the example below). It is often followed by a **cue** in small notes, showing what another instrument plays just before the entry:

## Ornaments

> **Acciaccatura** is pronounced a-chak-a-too-ra and **appoggiatura** is pronounced a-podge-a-too-ra.

Ornaments are short patterns of notes used to decorate a main note, each represented by a symbol or by grace notes (notes in small print that do not add to the count of beats in a bar). Ornaments were common in 17th- and 18th-century music, and trills and acciaccaturas are still used today.

| Example | Played as | Explanation |
|---|---|---|
|  |  | An **Acciaccatura** is played as quickly as possible before the main note, either on or just before the beat. |
|  | 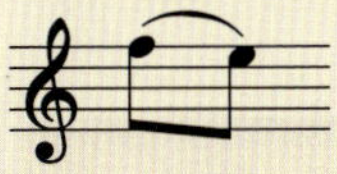 | An **appoggiatura** creates an expressive dissonance with the harmony, lasting for at least half the value of the main note. |
|  |  | A **mordent** is a rapid alternation of the main note with the note above (upper mordent) or note below (lower mordent). |
|  |  | A **trill** is a continuous alternation of the main note and the note above. The ending can vary. |
|  |  | A **turn** consists of the note above the main note, the main note itself, the note below and back to the main note again. |

Accidentals can be used with ornament signs, e.g.:

## KNOWLEDGE

### Other terms and signs

The passage in small notes below is an example of **fioritura**, a 'flowering' or decoration of the melodic line. These are often described as grace notes, even if they are not strictly ornamenting a main note. Composers may add the direction *ad lib.* to such passages, indicating that the rhythm can be treated quite freely.

*Chopin*

A wavy line before a chord indicates an **arpeggio**, meaning that the notes of the chord should be sounded in rapid succession rather than together. On instruments such as the piano or harp, each note is sustained until the end of the length of the written chord.

A wavy line between notes (or a straight line with the abbreviation *gliss.*) indicates a **glissando** or **slide** – a rapid glide from the first pitch to the next.

A small circle above a note (◦) instructs the performer of a string instrument to play a **harmonic** – a high, pure sound produced by lightly touching the string instead of using normal finger pressure.

The abbreviation **8ve** above the stave indicates that the bracketed music should be played an octave higher than written. Sometimes the figure 8 alone is used. If the bracket is below the stave, the music should be played an octave lower than written – sometimes the abbreviation **8ba** (ottava bassa) is used to confirm this.

For string and brass instruments, **con sordino** is an instruction to apply a mute, and **senza sordino** tells the player to remove it. Be careful not to confuse this with the term **muta**, which tells a musician to change something. For example, 'muta C in D' would be used to instruct a drummer to change the pitch of a kettledrum from C to D.

**Colla voce** ('with the voice') indicates that an accompaniment should follow the rhythm of the singer, which is likely to be flexible at this point.

**Segue** ('it follows') means 'continue straight on to the next section without a break'. The word **attacca** ('attach') has a similar meaning.

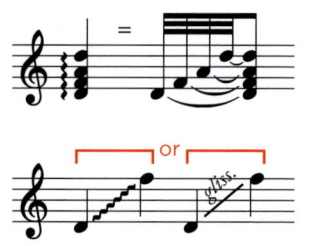

*A violin mute clipped to the bridge to dampen the sound*

### STEP UP

When writing about music for an exam, it is important to show that you understand and can use music terminology correctly. This includes knowing that tonality refers to keys (not tone) as well as understanding what texture means (see pages 56–57). Both points are often confused in exams.

Examiners will not be interested that you think a particular piece or composer is great or awful, although they may ask you what it is *in the music* that leads you to form such an opinion. You need to show what you know about the piece, using correct technical vocabulary, and you should always aim to answer the precise questions set.

# KNOWLEDGE

## Musical structures

The smallest structure in music is a **figure**, sometimes known as a **cell**. This melody is made mainly from repetitions of a four-note figure at different pitches:

*Debussy*

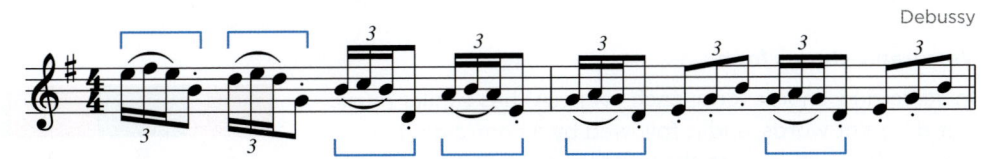

A **motif** is a short idea that is distinctive enough to retains its identity even when it is changed in various ways. In the next example, a three-note motif first spans a 4th, then a 5th, then a 9th. The last appearance is longer, but the motif's opening on a repeated G and ending with a ♩ ♪𝄾 rhythm are both recognisable:

**Allegro vivace**

*Schubert*

C:   I            Vb           Vb           I

The complete example above is a **phrase**, one of the basic building blocks of music. It is described as being four bars in length because its opening is balanced by only three beats in its last bar, making 16 beats in all. Phrases don't always end in a cadence, but there is usually some sense of a natural 'breathing point' in the musical flow, which may be confirmed by the use of **phrase marks** (long curved lines above or below the notes):

*Traditional*

Phrases are usually 2, 4 or 8 bars long, although other lengths are not uncommon. The essential thing is that a phrase forms a unit, like a spoken phrase.

The traditional melody above is an example of **periodic phrasing**, in which the first of two phrases of similar length sounds questioning and unfinished, because it ends on the dominant, while the second of the pair seems to supply an answer by ending on the tonic. These **balanced phrases** are a particular feature of music in the Classical period (see page 64). A melody that is the basis for part or all of a composition, may be described as a **theme**.

## Musical form

The shape or structure of a composition is known as its **form**. When explaining form, capital letters identify different sections of music, each usually consisting of a number of phrases, and numbers show variation. For example, ABA[1] indicates a first section (A), a new section (B) and a variant of the first section (A[1]).

---

**STEP UP**

Figures, cells, or motifs might make up a phrase. Phrases, in turn, might be grouped together in such a way as to make a melody. If the melody is used as the basis for a larger section of music, it can be described as a theme.

## KNOWLEDGE

### Strophic form

This is the simplest form, using the same tune for each verse of a song, as in a traditional blues or a Christmas carol. If a strophic song has three verses, the structure could be described as AAA.

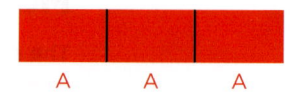

A  A  A

### Verse-and-chorus form

In verse-and-chorus form, each verse (A) has similar music but different words, and is followed by a contrasting chorus (B) in which both the words and the music are usually the same every time. The chorus may be repeated to make it all the more memorable.

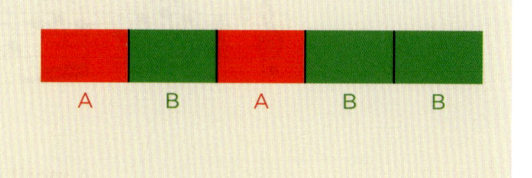

A  B  A  B  B

### Binary form

Binary form has two sections, each usually repeated, in the pattern ||: A :||: B :||. The second section is usually longer than the first, and the sections are often not very contrasted in content. The most important feature is that section A ends in a related key (the dominant if the main key is major, or the relative major if the main key is minor), while section B ends in the tonic. Binary form was often used for dances in the 17th and 18th centuries, and for short piano pieces in the 19th century.

A  B

### Ternary/Da capo form

Ternary form has three sections, the first of which returns at the end, either exactly (ABA) or varied (ABA$^1$). The B section usually contrasts with the A sections in key or content (or both). The repeat of the first section may be indicated by the term *da capo* at the end of the middle section, avoiding the need to write out the first section again. Many 18th-century songs do this and are consequently known as 'da capo' arias ('aria' being Italian for 'song').

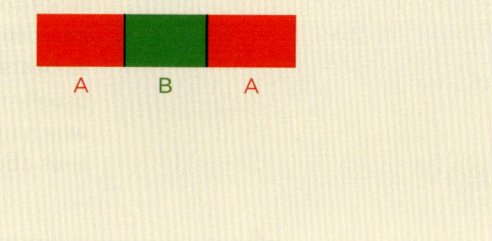

A  B  A

### Sonata form

Sonata form begins with a section called the **exposition**, in which a main theme called the first subject (labelled as 1 in the diagram) is heard in the tonic key. The music then moves to a closely related key, which often features a contrasting second subject (labelled as 2) in the new key. This material is transformed in various ways, and in a variety of keys, in a central section called the **development**. In the final section, called the **recapitulation**, material from the exposition returns, now all in the tonic key. The movement may end with a **coda** (closing passage) and sometimes there is a slow **introduction** before the start of the exposition.

1  2  1 1 2 2 1 2  1  2  coda

Exposition    Development    Recapitulation

### Rondo form

Rondo form is based on the idea of a rondo theme (A) that repeatedly comes around in the tonic key between contrasting episodes (B, C and so on) in related keys. This gives rise to structures such as ABACA or ABACADA.

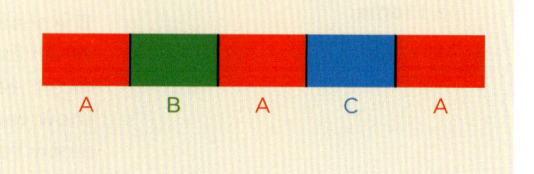

A  B  A  C  A

### Arch form

Arch form has a symmetrical structure such as ABCBA.

### Ritornello form

The 'ritornello' of the title refers to the opening section in the tonic key. Parts of the ritornello then return in related keys, separated by modulating episodes for one or more soloists. The final ritornello is in the tonic key. This differs from rondo form in that a rondo theme is normally complete and in the tonic every time it returns.

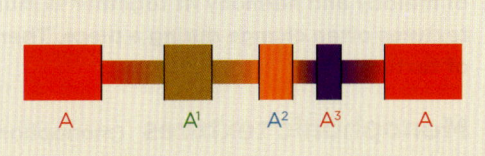

> **STEP UP**
>
> A particular category of music, such as the concerto or string quartet, can be described as a **genre**.

> Never describe music as a 'song' unless it is actually sung by a solo singer. Use terms such as 'piece' or 'work' if you don't have more precise details.

## Longer musical forms

Longer pieces of music often have several **movements**. These are substantial sections that are usually separated by short breaks in performance. They tend to be contrasted in mood but related in key, and individual movements are often in one of the forms listed in the previous section. Examples include:

- The **suite**: before 1750 the suite was a collection of short dances, mostly in binary form, sometimes preceded by a longer introductory movement entitled **overture** or **prelude**.

- The **concerto**: a type of music in which a soloist (or small group of soloists) is heard in contrast to, and in combination with, an orchestra. Most concertos have three movements, in the order fast–slow–fast.

- The **symphony**: the most common form of orchestral music from around 1750. Typically in four movements, in the order fast–slow–minuet–fast. The minuet was originally a dance in triple-time. It was replaced by the faster 'scherzo' in the 19th century. The slow movement might be in ternary form or a **theme and variations**. The last movement (or finale) might in rondo form, sonata form, or a combination of the two.

## Pop song structures

**Popular song form** developed from verse-and-chorus songs in the early 20th century. A short introduction replaces the first verse and the rest of the song consists of a repeated 32-bar chorus made from four eight-bar phrases in the pattern AABA. Each phrase has different lyrics, but the A phrases all have the same chord pattern and melody, sometimes based on a **hook** – a short, repeated melodic idea designed to stick in the memory. The B phrase, known as the 'middle eight' or 'bridge', has a contrasting tune with different harmonies, and lyrics that generally offer a different slant on the idea expressed in the A phrases.

Pop songs since the middle of the 20th century use a variety of structures but often have an extended verse-and-chorus form, in which there may be an introduction ('intro') at the start, an **instrumental** that substitutes for one of the sung verses, and a coda or 'outro' to provide a conclusion. The chorus may have an AABA structure, particularly in more old-fashioned songs. There may also be a **pre-chorus**, a short section that leads into the chorus proper, set to the same words each time it comes around.

## Texture

**The term texture refers to ways in which the simultaneous elements of melody and harmony fit together in music. Be aware that textures often change during a piece. There are three main kinds of texture.**

### Monophonic textures (monophonic = 'one sound')

An unaccompanied melody is described as a **monophonic** texture:

*Bach*

(unaccompanied cello)

Even if an unaccompanied melody is performed by a number of people in **unison** or in **octaves**, the texture is still described as monophonic.

### Homophonic textures (homophonic = 'same sounds')

A harmonised melody is described as a homophonic texture. It could be either

- a **chordal** texture, in which a melody is accompanied mainly by block chords:

*Beethoven*

- **melody and accompaniment**, in which the accompaniment does not have the same rhythm as the tune:

*Elgar*

### Polyphonic textures (polyphonic = 'many sounds')

Polyphonic or **contrapuntal** music has two or more simultaneous, independent melodies of roughly equal importance. Contrapuntal is the adjective used to describe **counterpoint** (another name for this type of texture). Each line is known as a **voice**, even if the piece is intended to be played rather than sung. The four voices in this example are identified by different colours:

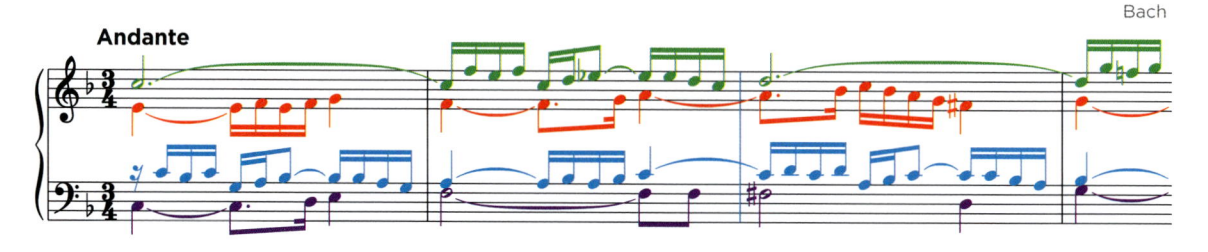

*Bach*

Counterpoint often features **imitation**, in which each part copies what has been played a few beats earlier by a previous part (whether at the same pitch or not), creating an overlap in the process:

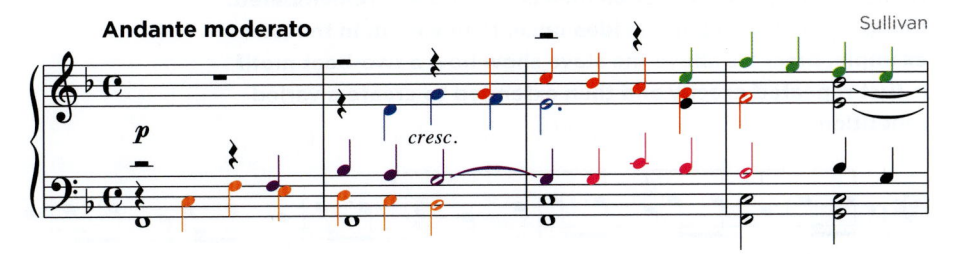

If the imitation is exact (which it is in the example below, but not in the one above) and it continues for some bars, the result is a **canon** and the texture is **canonic**:

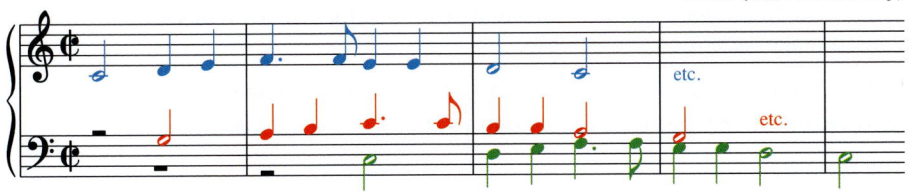

A **round** such as 'London's Burning' is a canon that continually repeats (think of going around and around).

## Other terms related to texture

The simultaneous performance of different versions of the same melody produces a **heterophonic** ('different sounds') texture:

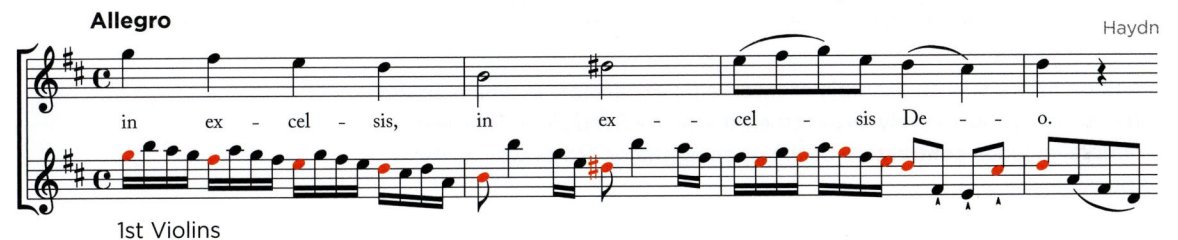

Heterophony is often heard in folk music when performers simultaneously decorate a melody in different ways. In classical music its effect is less obvious as it often appears as just one element within an overall homophonic texture.

In an **antiphonal** texture, two or more soloists or groups are separated to create a stereo-like effect when they alternate and combine.

A **layered** texture is a type of polyphony in which each voice consists of repetitive patterns rather than melodic lines. Typically, individual layers drop in and out of the overall texture to provide areas of contrast. Layered textures are a feature of some modern music written in a minimalist style, and are also found in some types of music from Africa and other world cultures.

A tune heard at the same time as a main melody, such as a descant sung above the melody of a traditional hymn or carol, is known as a **countermelody**.

A texture may be under-pinned by a **pedal** (see page 59).

### STEP UP

Texture can be described in general terms as thick or thin, but in exams it is preferable to be more precise (e.g. by describing the texture as two-part counterpoint).

## Compositional devices

Music happens in time and an idea is over in seconds, so **repetition** is important to ensure that an idea is noticed and remembered. Composers often repeat an idea once, then vary it. In the next example, brackets above the stave show how a two-beat motif is first repeated exactly and then extended to create a varied repetition:

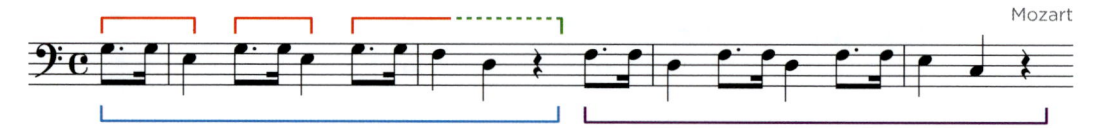

*Mozart*

The whole eight-beat phrase shown by the first bracket beneath the stave is then repeated a step lower in a device called **sequence** – the immediate repetition of an idea at a higher or lower pitch. It's a good way to make repetition sound fresh.

Melodic **variation** is another way to add interest when repeating an idea. Here is an example from Arban's *The Carnival of Venice*.

The main theme …

*Arban*

Becomes …

On page 53 we saw an example of **intervallic expansion**, in which an interval gets progressively larger (the melody by Schubert). The next example includes **contraction** of the opening major 3rd as well as its expansion:

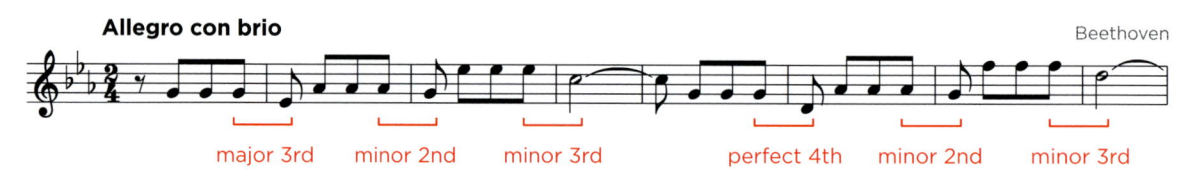

**Allegro con brio**  *Beethoven*

major 3rd   minor 2nd   minor 3rd   perfect 4th   minor 2nd   minor 3rd

**Fragmentation** is the result of breaking off part of a longer idea to develop independently:

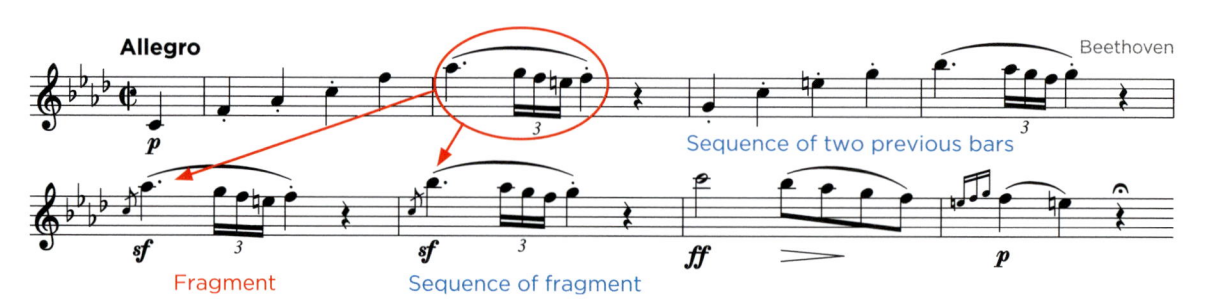

**Allegro**  *Beethoven*

Sequence of two previous bars

Fragment   Sequence of fragment

Notice that devices such as sequence do not have to be exact to make their point. The sequence in bars 3–4 above begins with a rising perfect 4th rather than the minor 3rd heard in bar 1, and it lacks an upbeat before this first rising interval.

# KNOWLEDGE

**Inversion** occurs if the intervals in a melody are turned upside down, so that rising intervals fall and falling intervals rise:

Becomes ...

**Augmentation** is an increase in the note lengths of a melody while **diminution** is a decrease. In the example below, stave 1 is a diminution of stave 3 and is an octave higher. Stave 2 is an augmentation of stave 3 and is a perfect 5th higher:

**Call and response** is a device often heard in jazz and world music, in which a solo phrase is immediately answered by one or more different performers.

The ostinato that dominates 'Mars' from *The Planets* by Holst

An **ostinato** (Italian for 'obstinate') is an idea that is repeated many times in succession, usually as an accompaniment to something else. The same device in electronic music is called a **loop**, and a similar device in rock and jazz is called a **riff**. A **ground bass** is an ostinato that repeats in the bass throughout an entire movement. The device was popular in English and Italian songs of the 17th century.

A **pedal** is a sustained or repeated note, usually in the bass, against which the harmony changes. If the pedal is above the harmony it is called an 'inverted' pedal. The term **drone** is used in folk music. A tonic pedal (see the top of page 57) creates a static effect while a dominant pedal generates excitement:

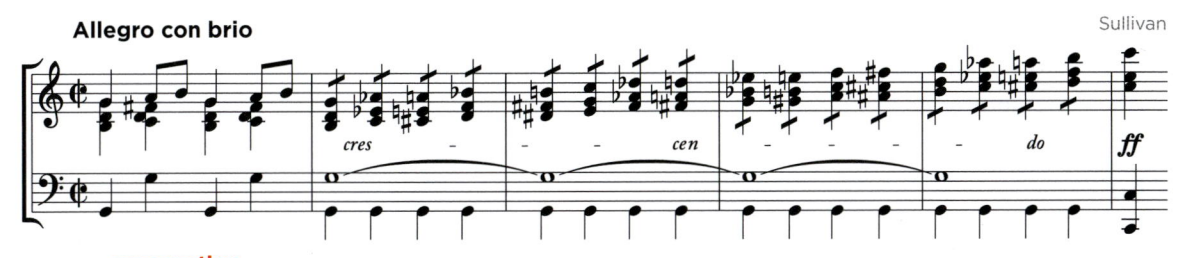

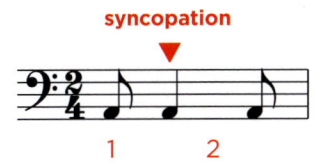

**syncopation**

**cross rhythm**

**Syncopation** occurs when notes off the beat are given prominence, temporarily upsetting the normal pattern of beats.

A **Cross rhythm** is produced when two conflicting rhythms are heard at the same time (as shown left).

COMPOSITIONAL DEVICES

## KNOWLEDGE

## Voices and instruments

### Voices

The four most common types of voice, from highest to lowest, are:

**soprano**   **alto**   **tenor**   **bass**

Soprano and alto parts are usually sung by women; tenor and bass parts are usually sung by men.

The small 8 below the tenor's treble clef is a reminder that a tenor voice sounds an octave lower than written. Most singers can manage a few notes beyond the ranges shown above, and professional singers usually have a range of at least two octaves.

A **treble** is a boy's voice with a range similar to a soprano. A **countertenor** (or **male alto**) is a high male voice with a range similar to that of an alto, usually produced by singing **falsetto** (the technique of using just the edge of the vocal cords to achieve a higher range than normal). A **mezzo-soprano** voice lies between soprano and alto in range. A **baritone** voice lies between tenor and bass in range.

When writing music, the text to be sung (called the **lyrics** in non-classical music) is split into separate syllables by hyphens, with each syllable positioned under the note (or first note) to which it is sung. When each syllable is set to a different note, the word setting is called **syllabic**. If a syllable is sung to several notes (called a **melisma**), the word setting is called **melismatic**.

> **STEP UP**
>
> **Range** (or **compass**) can apply to the music itself, as well as to the capabilities of a particular voice. So a song might have a wide range or a narrow range, or it might be set high or low within the singer's overall range.

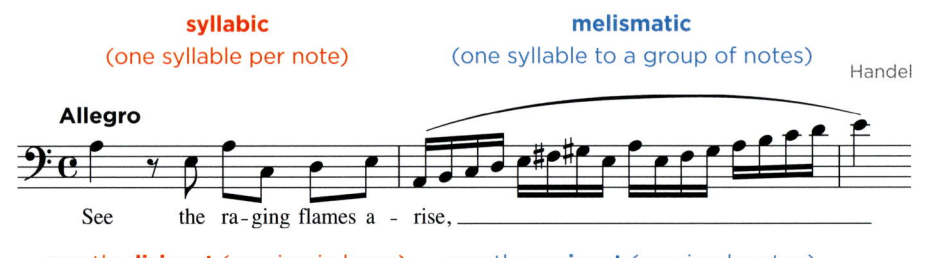

**syllabic**
(one syllable per note)

**melismatic**
(one syllable to a group of notes)

Handel

**Allegro**

See the ra-ging flames a - rise,

mostly **disjunct** (moving in leaps)   mostly **conjunct** (moving by step)

This example also illustrates **word painting**, which is the description in music of the words that are sung. Here, the tune rapidly ascends to illustrate the word 'arise'.

### Choirs

The most common type of **choir** (called a **chorus** in the theatre) is made up of all four voice types listed above. If a choir sings unaccompanied, it is known as singing **a capella**.

Choral music is usually laid out on four staves, bracketed together. There is one stave for each voice part, labelled with its capital letter (SATB). Simple choral music may be laid out on two staves, SA on one and TB on the other (which means that the tenor part is in the bass clef).

Stems usually point in opposite directions to differentiate the parts. Both of these examples sound the same:

*Sullivan*

> In the example above right, notice how notes must be written when parts on the same stave are in unison or just one step apart.

## Types of vocal music

**Opera** is a sung drama, presented on stage, in costume and to an instrumental accompaniment. Operas contain **arias** (the individual songs) and, in pre-20th century works, **recitative** – a type of solo vocal music that uses speech rhythms and lots of pitch repetition for moments when getting the words across is more important than melody. There are usually parts for a chorus, and sometimes dancers too.

An **operetta** is a light opera with spoken dialogue between the songs. It was the precursor of the **musical**, which often has more dialogue than music.

Types of solo song with piano accompaniment popular in the 19th century include the German **Lied** (plural, Lieder) and the generally slow and sentimental English **ballad**. Towards the end of the century, **Music Hall** songs became one of the main types of popular music.

An **oratorio** is a large-scale work for soloists, choir and orchestra, intended for concert performance. Most oratorios are on religious subjects. A **cantata** is a vocal composition in several movements, for one or more soloists with instrumental accompaniment and often including a choir. The text may be sacred or secular (non-sacred). Arias and recitatives are commonly found in oratorios and cantatas, as well as in opera. Choral music for church services includes settings of the Latin **mass** text in several sections, and single-movement, self-contained forms such as the **motet** (usually in Latin) and the **anthem**, which uses English words. **Plainsong** is a type of chant, traditionally performed in unison by unaccompanied men's voices.

The term **a cappella** ('in chapel style') is used for any type of unaccompanied singing, even if the music is secular (non-sacred) or pop music.

## The orchestra

The origins of the modern orchestra date from the 17th century, when a typical orchestral ensemble would consist of mainly string instruments. There was also a part for the **continuo** group, which would include at least one instrument (such as an additional cello) to reinforce the bass, and at least one chordal instrument (such as a harpsichord, organ or lute) to fill out the harmonies.

## KNOWLEDGE

By 1700, oboes and bassoons were regular members of orchestras. A flute was sometimes included, and trumpets and timpani were often added for ceremonial music. Nevertheless, orchestras seldom exceeded 18–24 players at this time.

By 1800 the wind section had expanded to pairs of flutes, oboes, clarinets, bassoons, horns and trumpets, plus timpani. More string players were needed to balance the wind, resulting in typically 40–50 players in all. The increased size meant that a keyboard instrument was no longer needed to fill out the harmonies.

By the late 19th century, most instruments had developed to their current state and the **symphony orchestra** had reached its modern size of at least 80 players:

> Before 1818 horns and trumpets had no valves, so could play only a limited selection of notes.

### The symphony orchestra

| | |
|---|---|
| woodwind | **2 flutes** and a **piccolo** (a small flute that sounds an octave higher than written)<br>**2 oboes** and a **cor anglais**\* (a large member of the oboe family)<br>**2 clarinets**\* and a **bass clarinet**\* (a large clarinet)<br>**2 bassoons** and a **contrabassoon** (a large bassoon that sounds an octave lower than written) |
| brass | **4 horns**\* (more are required for some works)<br>**3 trumpets**\*<br>**3 trombones** and a **bass trombone**<br>**1 tuba** |
| percussion | **timpani** (one player). These are kettledrums that can be tuned to specific pitches<br>**untuned percussion** (one or more players). Including instruments such as the side drum, bass drum, cymbals, triangle, tambourine, castanets and tam-tam (gong).<br>**tuned percussion** (usually one player). Including the xylophone, glockenspiel, celesta, marimba, vibraphone and tubular bells. |
| | **harp** (a small number of orchestral pieces also require a piano) |
| strings | **first violins** (approx. 14 players)<br>**second violins** (approx. 13 players)<br>**violas** (approx. 12 players). Violas use an alto clef in which the middle line represents middle C.<br>**cellos** (approx. 10 players). Cello is an abbreviation of 'violoncello'.<br>**double basses** (approx. 9 players). Double basses sound an octave lower than written. |

Instruments with a \* next to them are **transposing instruments**, which means that their notes do not sound at the pitches written. This has happened mainly for historical reasons, because it made the instruments easier to play in the early stages of their development.

Most transposing instruments are described as being 'in' a certain key, which is the note you hear when C is played, and most sound at a lower pitch than written. For example, a 'horn in F' sounds an F when C is written and played. From this you can work out that all of its notes sound a perfect 5th lower than written.

All the instruments below sound middle C when the notes shown are played.

Clarinet in B♭

Horn in F

Viola

**KNOWLEDGE**    63

Common transposing instruments are clarinets in A and in B♭, horns in F and trumpets in B♭. The cor anglais is not described as 'in F', but remembering that the name means 'English horn' will remind you that it is in F, just like the horn in F.

Orchestral scores are laid out in the order shown in the table on page 62, from woodwind at the top to strings at the bottom. Within each section the highest instruments are above the lower ones, except that horns appear at the top of the brass section in order to be close to the woodwind, with whom they often play.

A pair of wind instruments usually shares the same stave in an orchestral score. Stems point up for the first player and down for the second, and rests are positioned to show to which part they apply. The instruction **a 2** ('for two') tells both players to play the same notes.

If parts are playing the same notes in unison, we can say their parts are **doubled**. If they are playing the same notes an octave apart, they are 'doubling in octaves'.

String players can play two notes simultaneously (called **double stopping**). Triple and quadruple stopping are also possible. If string players are to divide into groups to play simultaneous notes, instead of using double-stopping, the instruction **divisi** (**div.**) is used. The instruction **unison** (**unis.**) or **non div.** indicates that everyone should now play the same notes.

Other instructions for strings include *pizzicato* (**pizz.**), which tells players that they should pluck the strings and *arco*, a direction to return to bowing the strings.

The Royal Scottish National Orchestra with Music Director Peter Oundjian

## Other instrumental ensembles

A **chamber orchestra** is a group of up to about 50 players that specialises in playing works written for smaller orchestras. A **string orchestra** is made up of only string players. Most of the instruments in a **brass band** differ from those in an orchestral brass section. They include cornets, flugelhorns, tenor horns and euphoniums, as well as trombones, three or four tubas and a percussion section. A **wind band** (or **concert band**) includes woodwind (with saxophones), brass and percussion. A **military band** is similar but plays while marching or (in a few cases) on horseback.

Smaller ensembles are often named after the type and number of instruments. For example, a **string quartet** consists of four stringed instruments (two violins, viola and cello) while a **brass quintet** consists of five brass instruments (usually two trumpets, horn, trombone and tuba). A **piano trio** consists of violin, cello and piano.

**Jazz bands** vary in size, but most include a **'horn section'** of saxophones, trumpet(s) and trombone(s) plus a **rhythm section** of piano, bass, drums and guitar or banjo. The bass could be a plucked upright bass (i.e. a double bass) or bass guitar.

The traditional configuration for a **rock band** is lead guitar (playing mostly melody lines), rhythm guitar (playing chords), bass guitar and drums, with one of the guitarists singing the lead vocal line. A keyboard player might substitute for one of the guitarists or be included as a fifth member of the band. Some guitarists read **tab** (short for tablature), which is a system of notation that shows finger positions on the neck of the instrument, using a six-line stave to represent the six strings. It is used mainly for lead guitar lines, while **guitar diagrams** are used for showing the finger positions of chords. Both are shown on the right.

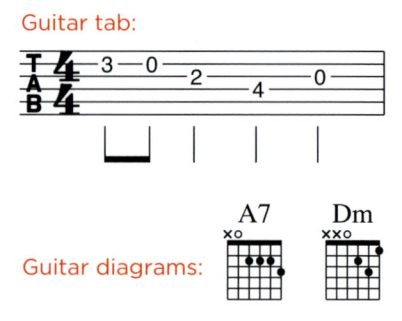

Guitar tab:

Guitar diagrams:

A typical rock band

## Historical periods

**The names of the periods into which western art music is divided are shared with other arts such as painting and literature. Dates are only a very approximate guide – new styles didn't appear overnight. It is important to realise that classical music is not the pop music of its day. It has always maintained a largely independent existence.**

Notice that Classical (with a capital C) refers only to one specific period within all of classical music. Also, remember how centuries are expressed: we are in the 21st century but each year begins with 20. Similarly, years in the 18th century begin with 17.

Although music has existed since the earliest times, we know little of how it sounded until monks developed a system of notation to preserve music for religious services. Much of the surviving music from the subsequent medieval period (1150–1450) was written for the church.

## Renaissance 1450–1600
- 'Renaissance' refers to a re-birth of the human spirit, and the age saw a new interest in secular (non religious) music, including madrigals, dance tunes, songs for voice with lute, and keyboard music.
- Church music remained important, with the Protestant reformation giving rise to new genres such as the German chorale (hymn) and English anthem.
- Composers include Josquin, Palestrina, Byrd and Victoria.

## Baroque 1600–1750
- This period begins with the invention of opera and before its end saw the foundation of the modern orchestra.
- Instrumental music became increasingly important, with new genres such as the sonata, suite and concerto.
- The sound of the harpsichord and exuberant contrapuntal textures are strong characteristics of the Baroque era.
- Composers include Monteverdi, Purcell, Vivaldi, Handel and Bach.

## Classical 1750–1825
- The Classical style emphasised clarity of line, elegance and melody-dominated homophony.
- The piano displaced the harpsichord as the keyboard instrument of choice while clarinets and horns helped swell the size of orchestras.
- Instrumental music included symphonies, concertos, string quartets and piano sonatas, and opera continued to grow in importance.
- Composers include Haydn, Mozart, Beethoven and Schubert.

## Romantic 1825–1900
- The Romantic style often emphasised emotional response in contrast to the balance and moderation of the Classical period.
- The orchestra reached its maximum size and virtuoso soloists dazzled audiences with their skill.
- New genres emerged, such as Lieder (German song) and the descriptive tone poem.
- Composers include Berlioz, Mendelssohn, Chopin, Schumann, Wagner, Verdi, Brahms, Saint-Saëns, Tchaikovsky, Grieg, Elgar and Puccini.

## Modern 1900–1975
- The early 20th century saw many diverse trends in music. Composers increasingly used dissonance, with some rejecting tonality entirely. Folk music, world music and jazz also became strong influences.
- Experimental approaches to composition included music formed through chance and the use of electronically generated sounds.
- Traditionalists continued to develop traditional forms, while music for film becomes a major force.
- Composers include Debussy, Vaughan Williams, Schoenberg, Bartók, Stravinsky, Gershwin, Copland, Shostakovich, Messiaen, Cage, Britten, Berio, Stockhausen, Birtwistle and Maxwell Davies.

## Postmodernism 1975 onwards
- Postmodernism means 'after modernism' and refers to a variety of styles.
- The best-known new development is minimalism, although composers continue to experiment in different directions.
- Composers have continued to write opera and music theatre pieces, although economics dictate that smaller-scale works often predominate. John Taverner, Arvo Pärt and Henryk Górecki (the 'holy minimalists') are noted for their spiritual approach to sacred music.
- Other composers include Ligeti, Steve Reich, Philip Glass, Michael Nyman, John Adams, Judith Weir and James MacMillan.

Composers are listed in order of their date of birth

# KNOWLEDGE

## Test your knowledge

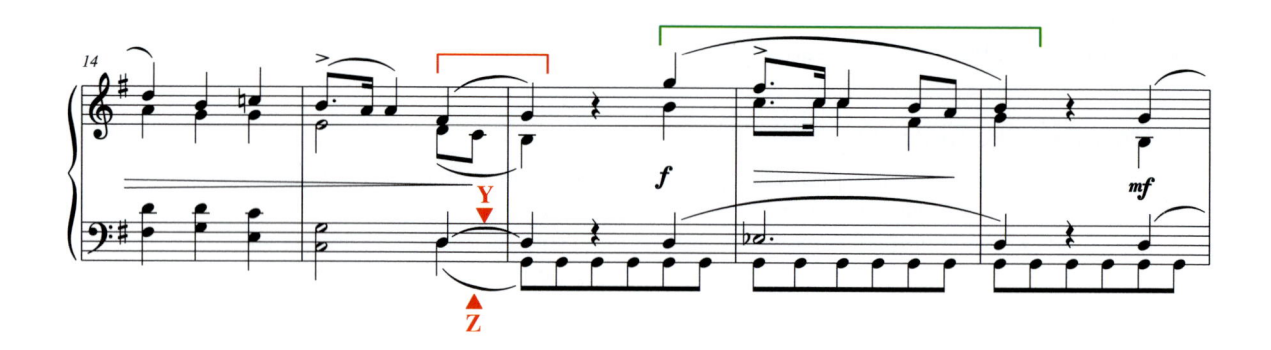

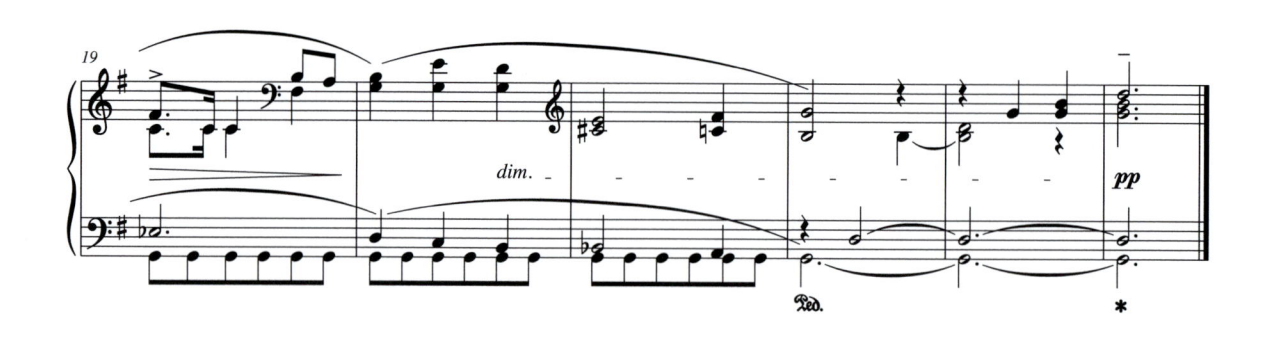

## ACTIVITY 22

Answer these questions about the piece of piano music printed opposite.

1. Give the meaning of each of the following:

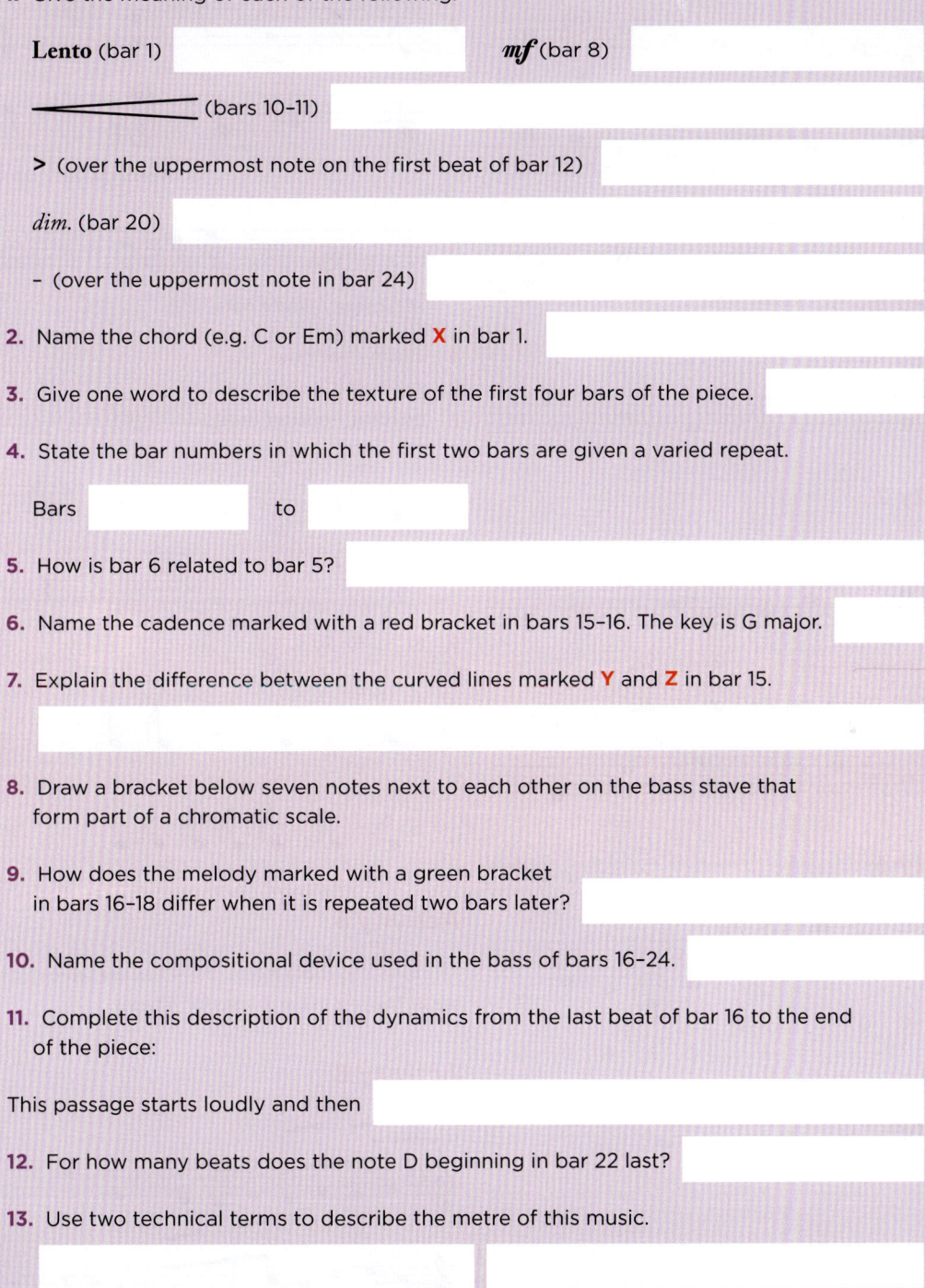

   **Lento** (bar 1) _____    *mf* (bar 8) _____

   ◁————— (bars 10–11) _____

   > (over the uppermost note on the first beat of bar 12) _____

   *dim.* (bar 20) _____

   – (over the uppermost note in bar 24) _____

2. Name the chord (e.g. C or Em) marked **X** in bar 1. _____

3. Give one word to describe the texture of the first four bars of the piece. _____

4. State the bar numbers in which the first two bars are given a varied repeat.

   Bars _____ to _____

5. How is bar 6 related to bar 5? _____

6. Name the cadence marked with a red bracket in bars 15–16. The key is G major. _____

7. Explain the difference between the curved lines marked **Y** and **Z** in bar 15.

   _____

8. Draw a bracket below seven notes next to each other on the bass stave that form part of a chromatic scale.

9. How does the melody marked with a green bracket in bars 16–18 differ when it is repeated two bars later? _____

10. Name the compositional device used in the bass of bars 16–24. _____

11. Complete this description of the dynamics from the last beat of bar 16 to the end of the piece:

    This passage starts loudly and then _____

12. For how many beats does the note D beginning in bar 22 last? _____

13. Use two technical terms to describe the metre of this music.

    _____    _____

14. This piece was composed in 1878. In what musical period is this? _____

# KNOWLEDGE

## Answers

### Activity 1

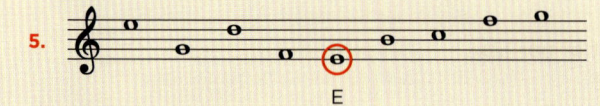

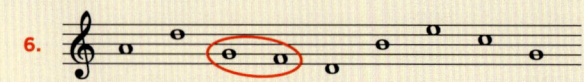

1. G
2. E
3. G
4. [staff notation] F
5. [staff notation] E
6. [staff notation]
7. DAD FED ED A BAD EGG
8. [staff notation]

### Activity 2

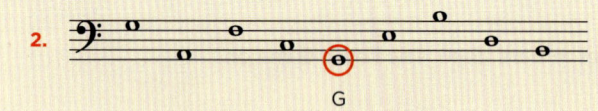

1. F
2. [bass clef staff notation] G
3. A DEAD BEE in her BAG on the BED
4. [bass clef staff notation]

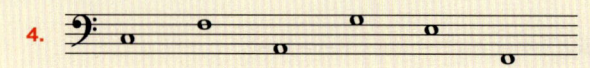

### Activity 3

1. [staff notation] C G B E D    C F B D G
2. [staff notation] (o)

### Activity 4

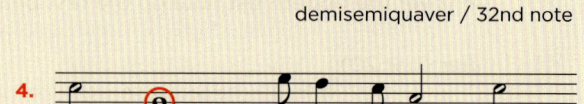

1. [staff notation]
2. [staff notation]
3. [staff notation] demisemiquaver / 32nd note
4. [staff notation] semibreve / whole note
5. minim / half note
6. semibreve / whole note
7. crotchet / quarter note
8. [rest notations]
9. (4 ½), 10, 6, 6, 5 ½
10. [rhythm notation]

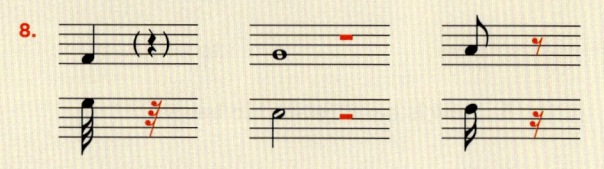

### Activity 5

This tune is in **triple** metre. Bar **4** has the same rhythm as bar **3**. The rest in bar **6** lasts for **3** beats.

### Activity 6

[music notation with "or" alternative]

### Activity 7

(free choice)

# KNOWLEDGE

## Activity 8

## Activity 9

1. D, G, A, B, B
2. E, B, B, B, E
3. 

## Activity 10

## Activity 11

1. 5th, 7th, 2nd, 1st, 3rd
   4th
2. dominant, tonic, submediant

## Activity 12

1. D flat, F sharp, A flat, D sharp
2. F sharp, D flat, C sharp, G flat

## Activity 13

3. F sharp, B, B flat, B / B natural

## Activity 14

1. F sharp, C sharp, E, E, C sharp F sharp
2. D major, 4, last bar:
3. A major, 3rd / mediant.

## Activity 15

1. B flat, A flat, D flat, C, E flat, F
2. E♭ major, 2, bar 4:
3. B♭ major.
   4th, 7th, 2nd
   3rd, 5th, 6th

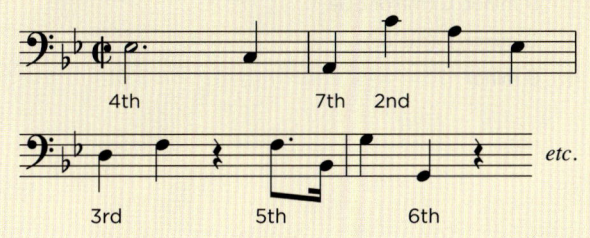

## Activity 16

1. (a) F♯  (b) A
2. (a) A♭  (b) F
3. B minor, 9
4.

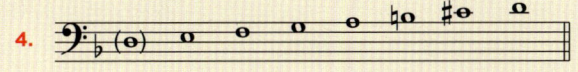

# KNOWLEDGE

## Activity 17

Major pentatonic, Mixolydian, Chromatic scale, Whole tone

## Activity 18

major 3rd, major 6th, minor 7th, perfect 4th, diminished 5th, minor 2nd

## Activity 19

1. (Key) F major, (Chord) tonic / F
2. G  D/F♯  G  Am/C  G/D  D⁷  G  or
   G (major):  I  Vb  I  iib  Ic  V⁷  I
3. Em  B/F♯  Em/G  B⁷/A  Em/G  Em  B  or
   E minor:  i  Vc  ib  V⁷d  ib  i  V
   Cm/E♭  D dim/F  G  Cm  or
   C minor:  ib  iib  V  i
4. A♭  Fm  D♭  B♭m  A♭  or
   A♭ major:  I  vi  IV  ii  I

## Activity 20

A major, plagal    G minor, interrupted
E minor, imperfect    D minor, perfect

## Activity 21

1. D minor, C (major), G♯
2. G minor, F (major)
3. B minor

## Activity 22

1. Very slow; moderately loud
   Gradually get louder
   Accent/emphasise the note or chord
   Gradually get quieter
   Hold/emphasise the note or chord
2. D
3. Chordal/homophonic
4. 9 to 10.
5. It is a descending (free) sequence
6. Perfect
7. Y is a tie, Z is a slur
8. Bar 11, beat 3 to bar 14, beat 1
9. It is an octave lower
10. (Tonic) pedal
11. Becomes gradually quieter until the end
12. 8
13. Simple triple
14. Romantic

(The music is the first piece in Tchaikovsky's Album for the Young Op.39)

# Index of terms

|  |  |
|---|---|
| Accents | 49 |
| Acciaccatura | 51 |
| Accidentals | 24–25 |
| Anacrusis | 13 |
| Antiphonal texture | 57 |
| Appoggiatura | 51 |
| Arco | 63 |
| Arpeggios | 38, 52 |
| Articulation marks | 49 |
| Attacca | 52 |
| Augmentation | 59 |
| Barlines | 12 |
| Baroque period | 65 |
| Bars | 12 |
| Bass clef | 7 |
| Beaming | 14–15 |
| Binary form | 54 |
| Broken chords | 38 |
| Cadences | 42 |
| Canon | 57 |
| Chords | 38–43 |
|   identifying chords | 40 |
|   progressions | 42–43 |
| Chord symbols | 39 |
| Chromatic | 35 |
| Circle of fifths | 30, 33, 43 |
| Classical period | 65 |
| Clefs | 5–7 |
| Coda | 51, 54, 55 |
| Compound time | 18 |
| Concerto | 55 |
| Conjunct | 60 |
| Contraction | 58 |
| Contrapuntal texture | 56 |
| Crescendo | 48 |
| Cross rhythm | 59 |
| Crotchet | 9–10 |
| Da capo | 50 |
| Da capo form | 54 |
| Degrees of the scale | 23 |
| Demisemiquaver | 9–10 |
| Diatonic | 35 |
| Diminished intervals | 36–38 |
| Diminuendo | 48 |
| Diminution | 59 |
| Disjunct | 60 |
| Dotted notes | 10 |
| Duple metre | 12 |
| Duplet | 19 |
| Dynamics | 48 |
| Eighth note | 9–10 |
| Enharmonic equivalents | 24, 37 |
| Figuration | 38 |
| Form | 53–55 |
| Fragmentation | 58 |
| Glissando | 52 |
| Half note | 9–10 |
| Harmonics | 52 |
| Harmony | 38–43 |
| Heterophony | 57 |
| Homophony | 56 |
| Imitation | 57 |
| Intervallic expansion | 58 |
| Intervals | 36–37 |
| Inversion (of melody) | 59 |
| Inversions (of chords) | 38–40 |
| Keys | 26–33 |
| Key signatures | 26–33 |
| Leger lines | 8 |
| Major keys | 26–30 |
| Melisma | 60 |
| Metre | 18–19 |
|   simple time | 18 |
|   irregular metre | 18 |
|   compound time | 18 |
| Minim | 9–10 |
| Minor keys | 31–33, 39 |
| Modes | 34–35 |
| Modulation | 44–46 |
| Motif | 53 |
| Ornaments | 51 |
| Ostinato | 59 |
| Pedal | 59 |
| Phrasing | 53 |
| Pizzicato | 63 |
| Polyphonic texture | 56 |
| Postmodernism | 65 |
| Prelude | 55 |
| Quadruple metre | 12 |
| Quarter note | 9–10 |
| Quaver | 9–10 |
| Renaissance period | 65 |
| Repeats | 50–51 |
| Repetition | 50 |
| Rests | 9–11, 13, 16, 51 |
| Riff | 59 |
| Ritornello form | 55 |
| Romantic period | 65 |
| Rondo form | 54 |
| Scales | 22–23, 26–35 |
|   blues | 35 |
|   chromatic | 35 |
|   C major | 22 |
|   hexatonic | 34 |
|   pentatonic | 34 |
| Semibreve | 9–10 |
| Semiquaver | 9–10 |
| Semitone | 21 |
| Sequence | 58 |
| Seventh chords | 39 |
| Simple time | 18 |
| Sixteenth note | 9–10 |
| Slash chord | 39 |
| Slur | 49 |
| Sonata form | 54 |
| Staccatissimo | 49 |
| Staccato | 49 |
| Stave | 4 |
| Strophic form | 54 |
| Symphony | 55 |
| Syncopation | 59 |
| Tempo | 47 |
| Ternary form | 54 |
| Texture | 56–57 |
| Theme | 53 |
| Time signatures | 12–13, 18–19 |
| Tonality | 44–46 |
| Tone | 21 |
| Transposing instruments | 62 |
| Treble clef | 5 |
| Triads | 38–39 |
| Trill | 51 |
| Triple metre | 12 |
| Triplets | 17 |
| Tuplets | 17 |
| Turn | 51 |
| Variation | 58 |
| Whole note | 9–10 |

## FURTHER READING

### About the author:

**PAUL TERRY** studied music at the University of East Anglia and trained as a teacher at Cambridge University. He taught from primary to 6th-form level for 20 years, including 15 years as head of music at a well-known public school, after which he combined examining with part-time teaching at his local university.

Paul was an examiner for the Associated Board of the Royal Schools of Music for nearly 30 years, and has been Chief Examiner in Music for both OCSEB (now part of OCR) and Edexcel (for whom he pioneered the introduction of Music Technology as an A-level subject). He has also served as a member of the Secondary Examinations Council and its successor the Schools Examinations and Assessment Council, and has been employed as a music consultant by several examining boards.

---

### Available from Rhinegold Education for your course:

**GCSE Study Guide**
(for AQA, Edexcel and OCR exam boards)

**GCSE Listening Tests**
(for AQA, Edexcel, OCR and WJEC/Eduqas exam boards)

**GCSE Revision Guide**
(for AQA, Edexcel, OCR and WJEC/Eduqas exam boards)

### You may find the following books useful too:

Go to www.rhinegoldeducation.co.uk for a complete list of our resources.

**GCSE Music Composition Workbook**

**GCSE Music Literacy Workbook**

**GCSE Performance Pieces:**
Piano, Voice, Alto Sax, Clarinet, Flute, Guitar, Bass Guitar, Drums

**Understanding Popular Music**

**Careers in Music**

**Music Technology from Scratch**

**Dictionary of Music in Sound**

---

You should always check the current requirements of your examination, since these may change.

Rhinegold Education has used its best efforts in preparing this guide. It does not assume, and hereby disclaims,
any liability to any party for loss or damage caused by errors or omissions in the guide whether such errors or omissions result from negligence, accident or other cause.